TOUR OF TOURS

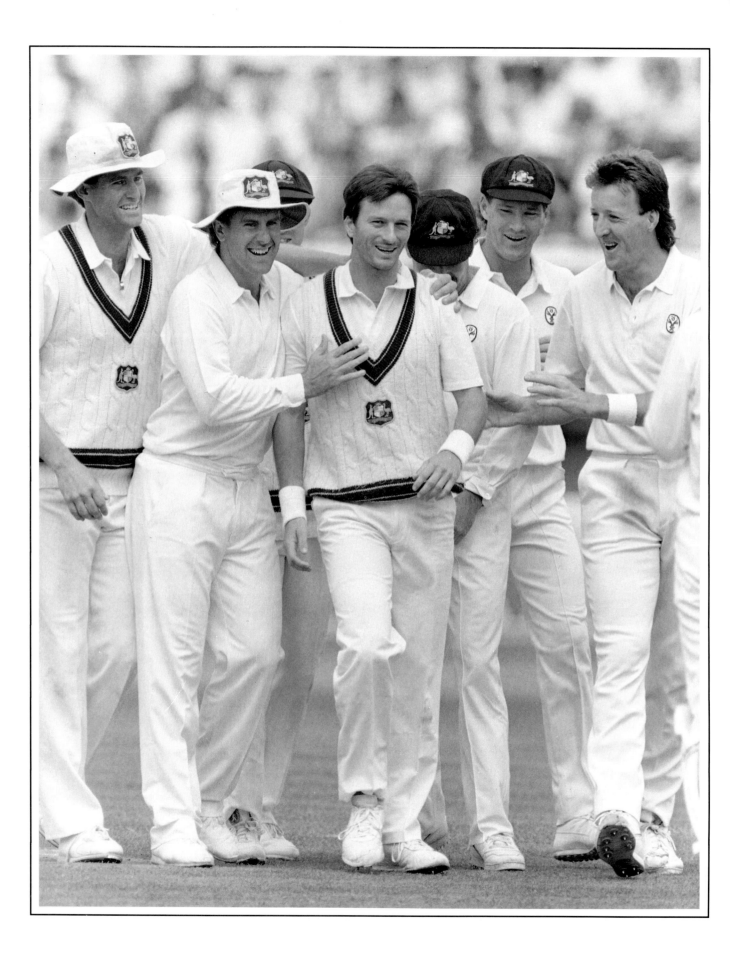

TOUR OF TOURS

Border's victorious Australians of 1989

PATRICK EAGAR and ALAN ROSS

HODDER AND STOUGHTON
SYDNEY LONDON AUCKLAND TORONTO

FOR TESSA

British Library Cataloguing in Publication Data

Eagar, Patrick
1. England. Cricket. English teams. Test matches,
1989 with Australian teams. Cricket. Australian teams.
Test matches, 1989 with English teams.
I. title   II. Ross, Alan *1922–*
796.35′865

ISBN 0;340-50286-X

First published 1989

Published by Hodder and Stoughton,
a division of Hodder and Stoughton Ltd,
Mill Road, Dunton Green, Sevenoaks, Kent TN13 2YE
Editorial office: 47 Bedford Square, London WC1B 3DP

Photoset by Rowland Phototypesetting (London) Ltd

Printed in Hong Kong by Colorcraft Ltd.

Book designed by Trevor Spooner

*Acknowledgement. Patrick Eagar would like to acknowledge
the patient and skilful assistance throughout this book
of Jan Traylen and in particular his aerial photograph
of The Oval in the colour section.*

*Frontispiece – Steve Waugh surrounded by delighted team-mates
after taking a wicket in the Third test at Edgbaston.*

Contents

Introduction

England, for the first time in some years, had the winter off, though the matter was not of their choosing. There were rumours of a more professional approach to the handling of Test team preparation and selection, Peter May having resigned in the autumn after a fairly torrid summer. In due course, after some muttered objections, Edward Dexter was appointed Chairman of Selectors, a post now salaried, which was something his predecessors had neither required nor enjoyed.

Dexter was soon in action, initially by way of press conferences and then, as the season developed, by lightning visits to the county grounds. These he made, despite an operation to a heel that put him for a while on crutches, by motorbike and car, a demonstration of enthusiasm and interest that was impressive.

The first break with tradition was the appointment of David Gower as captain, not just for one Test but for the whole summer. This contrasted agreeably with 1988, when England called on five captains and in the end had nothing to show for it. But then West Indies were their opponents.

Dexter began to lay down plans for ensuring no player would bat or bowl to Test match standard undetected. A group of regional observers, all former Test players, was announced: David Brown and Bob Willis to attend to the bowling; Arthur Milton and Philip Sharpe to the batting; Alan Knott and Bob Taylor to run an eye

Allan Border. Record to May 1989.
As batsman. *102 Tests: 179 innings; not out 30; 7831 runs; highest score 205; average 52.55 (including 23 hundreds, and 37 fifties).*
As captain. *39 Tests: 7 wins, 13 losses, 18 drawn, 1 tie*
(Figures, courtesy Richard Lockwood.)

over their fellow wicket-keepers.

The Australians, hard-worked and fairly unsuccessful over recent months against the West Indies and Pakistan, were nevertheless the World champions at one-day cricket. Their arrival in England coincided with an astonishingly brilliant spring and early summer, and they lost scarcely any opportunities for net practice or play against the counties. They had their setbacks – Sussex beat them in a one-day match at Hove and Worcestershire on a bad wicket in a three-day match at Worcester – but these were of trifling importance compared to the running into form of their main batsmen. Boon was bursting with runs, as was Jones despite suffering a fractured cheekbone at the hand of Pigott. The newcomers Taylor and Veletta were less fortunate, but there was more than enough evidence that Australia, with Border and Waugh in the middle of the order and Marsh as a prolific and composed partner for Boon as an opener, were going to be a difficult side to bowl out.

Their bowling was another matter. Lawson, Rackemann, Alderman and Hughes were all of modest pace compared to their West Indian counterparts, and the spin, divided between May and Hohns, seemed of a quality unlikely to cause trouble. In Waugh, though, Australia possessed a talented all-rounder whose performances it would be interesting, as the summer wore on, to compare with Pringle and a much reduced Botham.

David Gower. Record to May 1989.
As batsman. *100 Tests: 172 innings; not out 13; 7000 runs; highest score 215; average 44.02 (including 14 hundreds, and 35 fifties).*
As captain. *26 Tests: 5 wins, 14 losses, 7 drawn*
(Figures, courtesy Richard Lockwood.)

Gower opens

Allan Border and David Gower shake on it. The series began in friendly fashion and there was every reason to believe it would stay that way. The weather from the outset had been welcoming and most of the newcomers were in some sort of form.

Australia arrived as champions of the one-day game, England held the Ashes. The reverse of that seemed more than likely by the end of June.

After weeks of sunshine and the temperature hovering in the upper seventies Old Trafford contrived to be overcast and sunless. But Gower, having won the toss, had no hesitation in batting. He decided to open the innings himself with Gooch and at once launched an attack on Lawson. Several times he leaned him sweetly past mid-off and slashed him fine of cover. When Lawson pitched short Gower pulled for six over square leg, 55 runs coming off the first eleven overs.

This opening assault was a happy signalling of intent; but England rather lost their way in mid-afternoon when Lawson bowled excellently in his second spell and Rackemann gave him good support.

It was Rackemann who got Gower out in the old way, slanting the ball across him and finding the edge. Gatting did not last long, lobbing the ball off his aerated pads via his bat to an astonished Boon at cover. Then Gooch, having batted all morning without a semblance of doubt, got himself out to Border, mistiming a sweep, in the last over before lunch. Appetite seemed to have unhinged him.

Gower's decision to go in first was influenced by his wish to get Robin Smith, in fine form for Hampshire, in at no. 5. This soon bore fruit, for Smith was quickly into his stride, overhauling a curiously stodgy Lamb. Lamb in fact batted eighty minutes for 35, hitting no boundaries, while Smith, in half the time, scored the same number of runs and hit four boundaries.

From 160 for 3 England subsided to 179 for 6, the impetus being lost just when the afternoon promised most. Lamb chopped Lawson on to his stumps and then Botham, having managed only three rather tentative strokes in twelve balls, sliced Lawson hard at the ample bosom of Boon at backward point.

Runs were now hard to come by and earlier visions of a total in the region of 275 had to be hastily adjusted. Pringle and Rhodes found it difficult to pierce the field and only some ballooning drives by De-Freitas and some last-over fielding confusion got England as far as 231 for 9 in their 55 overs.

Although this was no great total the slowness of the pitch and outfield meant that it would take some getting. In fact Australia's chances were blown away in just over half an hour, by which time they were 17 for 3. Boon, in humming form all May, drove rather euphorically at DeFreitas, a ball of full length slipping between bat and pad to uproot his off stump. Jones glanced Foster over-delicately and was caught down the leg side by Rhodes. Then, crucially, Foster found an absolute beauty for Border, the ball nipping back at him to hit the off stump.

There was really no recovering from this and much of the interest went out of the proceedings. Embury came on to bowl tidily and get both turn and wickets. Marsh was virtually stagnant, managing only 17 runs in 92 minutes, before Embury had him caught off bat and pad. Waugh lasted long enough and batted ably enough to suggest there might be a glimmer of

England won the toss

ENGLAND

G. A. Gooch c Jones b Border	52
*D. I. Gower c Healy b Rackemann	36
M. W. Gatting c Boon b Waugh	3
A. J. Lamb b Lawson	35
R. A. Smith c and b Alderman	35
I. T. Botham c Boon b Lawson	4
D. R. Pringle lbw b Waugh	9
†S. J. Rhodes b Lawson	8
P. A. J. DeFreitas not out	17
J. E. Embury b Rackemann	10
N. A. Foster not out	5
Extras (lb 12, w 3, nb 2)	17

Total (for 9 wkts, 55 overs) ... **231**

Fall of wickets: 1-55, 2-70, 3-125, 4-161, 5-167, 6-179, 7-190, 8-203, 9-220

Bowling: Alderman 11-2-38-1; Lawson 11-1-48-3; Rackemann 10-1-33-2; Waugh 11-1-45-2; Moody 8-0-37-0; Border 4-0-18-1

AUSTRALIA

G. R. Marsh c Rhodes b Embury	17
D. C. Boon b DeFreitas	5
D. M. Jones c Rhodes b Foster	4
*A. R. Border b Foster	4
S. R. Waugh c Smith b DeFreitas	35
T. M. Moody b Embury	24
M. R. J. Veletta lbw b Pringle	17
†I. A. Healy c Embury b Foster	10
G. F. Lawson c DeFreitas b Embury	0
C. G. Rackemann b Botham	6
T. M. Alderman not out	0
Extras (b 1, lb 9, w 4)	14

Total (47.1 overs) ... **136**

Fall of wickets: 1-12, 2-13, 3-17, 4-64, 5-85, 6-115, 7-119, 8-120, 9-136

Bowling: Foster 10-3-29-3; DeFreitas 8-3-19-2; Pringle 8-2-19-1; Botham 10.1-1-28-1; Embury 11-0-31-3

Umpires: J. W. Holder and N. T. Plews

Man of the match: P. A. J. DeFreitas

Result: England won by 95 runs

response, but DeFreitas eventually had him taken at deep mid-wicket. Botham, who had not bowled at all badly, pitching the ball up and getting some swing, finished things off by rattling Rackemann's stumps.

England had looked brisk and energetic in the field and they were not flattered by their margin of victory. The sun finally emerged, but not before impatient spectators, deprived of their quota of big hits, scattered torn-up bits of paper resembling confetti over the ground. The only chance Australia had was the match being brought to a halt by drifting paper.

For England it had been an efficient sweep by the new broom, but the precedent of 1988, in relation to the Tests, meant that any justified enthusiasm needed to be tempered.

Robin Smith during his innings of 25. His hair might have recalled an old-time movie star but he brought a healthy note of aggression to England's batting.

DeFreitas bowls Boon for 5. All May Boon had thrived on county bowling, almost to saturation point. This time he drove somewhat airily, and the flying stump was even more of a surprise to him than to the bowler.

First One-day International Old Trafford

Steve Waugh during his innings at Old Trafford. He only made 35, but it was enough to make him Australia's top scorer. The perfection of this stroke – the position of head and feet, the balance of the body, the follow-through – was repeated hundreds of times this summer.

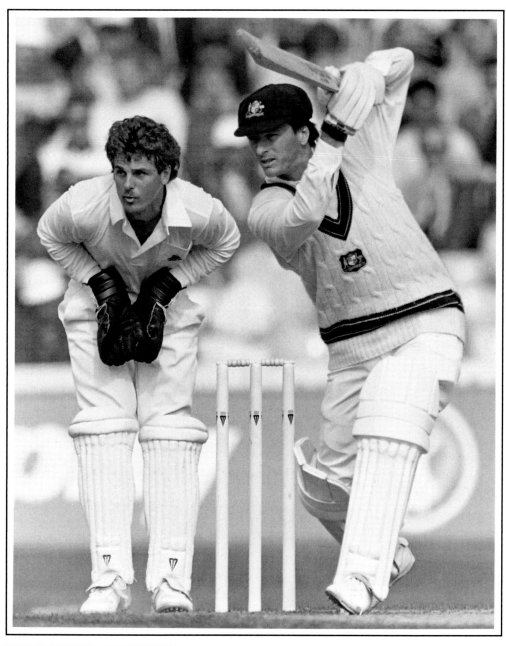

Emburey picked up three wickets for 31 in his eleven overs and this was one of them, Marsh being caught by the wicket-keeper, Rhodes.

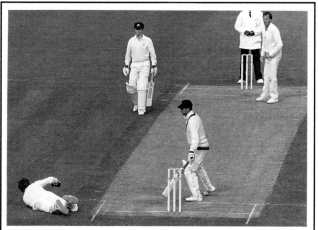

When is a tie not a tie?

None of the Manchester cloud cover sailed down to Trent Bridge. Gower again won the toss and he and Gooch went out to bat under a sky of unremitting blue. Australia's new-ball attack had learned lessons in direction from Old Trafford and Gower, once again intent on establishing a psychological dominance, was only able to progress through airy slashes to the third-man boundary. Gooch was more circumspect but his first attempt at clearing the leg-side ring ended in a high catch to Jones. With the score 57 Gower, given no room for his favoured square drive, cut at one too close to him from Waugh and dragged the ball on to his wicket.

Gatting and Lamb made fair progress, though Gatting thus far seemed somewhat reduced in authority. The introduction of May's off-spinners, the kind of bowling that generally makes Gatting salivate, this time had an opposite effect. First Gatting drove over a yorker and then, in the next over, Smith went down the pitch, missed, and was stumped, Healy having initially failed to gather the ball.

Worse was to come, for Botham, at the crease only a few minutes, was sent back by Lamb, Border hitting the stumps at the bowler's end with Botham stranded.

At 138 for 5, with a dozen overs left, England looked to have ruined their chances. Lamb, however, thrives on this kind of situation and he now began to savage the bowling. Anything on a length

Gower, bowled Waugh, 28. Another sight often to be repeated, Gower cutting at one too close to the stumps and of too full a length and dragging the ball on to his wicket.

England won the toss

ENGLAND

G.A. Gooch c Jones b Alderman	10
*D.I. Gower b Waugh	28
M.W. Gatting b May	37
A.J. Lamb not out	100
R.A. Smith st Healy b May	3
I.T. Botham run out	8
D.R. Pringle not out	25
Extras (lb 14, w 1)	15
Total (for 5 wkts, 55 overs)	**226**

†S.J. Rhodes, P.A.J. DeFreitas, J.E. Emburey and N.A. Foster did not bat

Fall of wickets: 1-30, 2-57, 3-119, 4-123, 5-138

Bowling: Alderman 9-2-38-1; Lawson 11-0-47-0; Rackemann 11-1-37-0; Waugh 11-1-47-1; May 11-1-35-2; Moody 2-0-8-0

AUSTRALIA

D.C. Boon c Botham	28
G.R. Marsh lbw b Emburey	34
D.M. Jones b Emburey	29
*A.R. Border c Rhodes b Pringle	39
S.R. Waugh run out	43
T.M. Moody run out	10
†I.A. Healy not out	26
G.F. Lawson c Gooch b Foster	1
T.B.A. May b DeFreitas	2
C.G. Rackemann not out	0
Extras (b 1, lb 6, w 7)	14
Total (for 8 wkts, 55 overs)	**226**

T.M. Alderman did not bat

Fall of wickets: 1-59, 2-81, 3-116, 4-153, 5-174, 6-205, 7-218, 8-225

Bowling: Foster 11-2-44-1; DeFreitas 11-0-48-1; Pringle 11-1-38-1; Botham 11-0-42-1; Emburey 11-0-47-2

Umpires: H.D. Bird and J.H. Hampshire

Man of the match: A.J. Lamb

Result: A tie

Second One-day International Trent Bridge

Gatting out after making 37, a score he came nowhere near to equalling for several weeks. It was not one of Gatting's more authoritative innings and, as the early season progressed he grew more an more out of form, for Middlesex as well as for England. Niggling injuries did not help.

he hit on the up, over extra-cover or past the bowler's head, anything short he crashed past gully or pulled to mid-wicket. Pringle did better than usual in keeping up with him and together they put on 88 without being parted. Lamb reached his hundred – his fourth in one-day internationals – off the last ball of the innings, Alderman's last two overs costing 26 runs.

Australia this time got off to a better start, helped by Botham putting down a comparatively easy chance at slip. Foster was the bowler and Marsh, then 5, the batsman. From now on Australia were always slightly ahead of England, though wickets fell just when they appeared most in control. At 59 Boon hit over a gentle in-swinger from Botham, at 81 Marsh was lbw to Emburey, and at 116 Jones, looking menacing, changed his mind in mid-stroke and was bowled by Emburey.

Now Border and Waugh began to move along nicely, the rate required remaining steady around the six-per-over mark. Pringle returned to pin down Border, his slower ball deceiving him and finding the edge – a reward for bowling of much thoughtfulness.

Australia were now 153 for 4, some 20 runs ahead of England at the same stage. Moody hit a huge six over mid-wicket but declined a more than reasonable call by Waugh and was run out. Waugh continued to prosper, mainly at Emburey's expense, but lost his wicket in a most cruel fashion. Going for a harmless-looking third run, he arrived at the crease only to find Healy had slipped on turning and was stalled at the same end.

That was 205 for 6, with 22 runs still wanted to win. With three overs to go Australia needed 18 and, after the next over, 12. Gooch took a blinding catch at deep cover to remove Lawson; and with De-Freitas to bowl the final over Australia required 7.

DeFreitas began with a wide followed by two full tosses. His fifth ball bowled May. Rackemann, with two runs needed, had the chance to make history of a sort, but DeFreitas' final delivery whirred past his off stump. Healy, a pulled muscle notwithstanding, tore up the pitch in the wake of the ball and flung himself full-length to beat Rhodes' throw from behind the stumps. A lob to the other end, with a fielder in position to gather the throw, must have run Rackemann out by half a pitch's length.

A tie, however, it was, and perhaps the most fitting end to a match of many excitements. It turned out, to the surprise of most people, that whoever won at Lord's the Texaco Trophy would go to England, on account of their having lost fewer wickets – five as against eight – in the tied match. When the rules were laid down, it can scarcely have seemed likely that this particular one would be called into question.

England 138 for 5, and only 12 overs left. But Allan Lamb likes this kind of challenge. He reached his hundred off the last ball of the innings, treating Alderman with a disdain no-one ever repeated. This was Lamb's fourth hundred in one-day internationals, a species of cricket in which he has few equals.

Second One-day International Trent Bridge

(Right) *Allan Border kept the Australian innings ticking over, so that the run rate was always close to the target. He is a master at pacing an innings, without ever seeming to hurry. He is a good judge of a run and he makes sure his partner runs with him.*

(Below and across) *Two overs to go and Australia need 12 to win. Gooch, in the deep, takes a magnificent catch to remove Lawson, his final position a laudable likeness to that of the dying swan at the end of Tchaikovsky's ballet.*

(Left) Moody became the second victim in a flurry of run-outs. You couldn't see him for dust.

(Below) Healy was given a runner, but when he arrived he forgot him, to the extent of covering the ground even faster than Dean Jones could. As a result Gower, not unnaturally, queried the necessity.

Second One-day International Trent Bridge

The last ball, and the injured Healy flies down the pitch, making his ground with his partner, Rackemann, only half way to his. So the match was tied. Everyone seems to be appealing, since the wicket-keeper, standing back, hit the stumps. A throw to the other end might have done more good. As it turned out, a tie was enough for England, through losing fewer wickets, to take the Texaco Trophy.

A high-scoring match

This was always going to be a high-scoring match, with Lord's looking at its best, the ground full, and the weather perfect. Although pitch and outfield were likely to quicken up as the day went on, Gower, winning the toss for the third time in a row, decided to bat. Once again England got off to a fluent start. The Australian bowling was respectably tidy but Gooch and Gower had few problems, each of them scoring freely down their favoured avenues. Gower was the first to go, at 123, an opening partnership that laid the ground for steady acceleration. This, however, never fully materialised, with Gatting, despite some effective cutting, being unusually confined and Lamb lbw to his first ball. Smith, though, looked in good form, driving with a flourish and revving up the running between the wickets.

Gooch was his solid self, but there remained a suspicion that England were never quite scoring fast enough to make the game safe. In the scurry of the final few overs wickets fell, Gooch's amongst them, and it was left to Botham, who made 25 off the eleven balls he received, to give the fairly staid proceedings a dash of adventure.

Australia, in their reply, were always just ahead of England, though Marsh took an hour or so to liven up. Boon was lbw to Foster for 19, and at 84 Jones was well taken by Gower off Emburey. This brought Border in, and as long as he was there, the target seemed well within Australia's sights.

Border scored off almost every ball, reaching 50 off only 40 deliveries. He dabbed, cut and drove, and it was a shock when he hit over a shortish ball from Pringle, which he attempted to pull.

This was an important wicket for England, with Australia still needing 81 at just over seven runs an over. The responsibility was now on Marsh and he at once began to lap good-length balls over mid-wicket. Emburey dropped him twice there, one fiendishly difficult, one fairly straightforward. Waugh was not idle either, and when Foster returned for his final spell, he struck two sixes off successive balls into the Tavern stand.

The partnership between Marsh and Waugh, making 71 off 57 balls, turned an awkward task into a comparatively comfortable one. Waugh was splendidly caught by Gooch at long-on but by then only 10 runs were needed at a run a ball. Off the last over Australia needed 5, and they got these with three balls left.

England had bowled far too much down the leg side. Marsh, taking his time, had seemed on occasion to be less ambitious than was warranted, but he took over from Border and in due course Waugh took over from him.

Both sides had fielded splendidly and though the trophy had already gone to England the tension lasted to the very end. It seemed a fine augury for the Test matches.

Gooch (above) and Gower gave England a splendid start of 123, but though Gooch remained almost to the end the innings sagged slightly in the middle. Gatting was often contained and Lamb was out first ball.

Gary Lineker, England's centre forward and no mean cricketer himself, looks on from the players' balcony. Botham, too, gets a brief look-in, his innings of 11 balls producing 25 runs.

England won the toss

ENGLAND

G.A. Gooch b Alderman	136
*D.I. Gower c Veletta b Moody	61
M.W. Gatting run out	18
A.J. Lamb lbw b Alderman	0
R.A. Smith b Rackemann	21
I.T. Botham not out	25
P.A.J. DeFreitas c Rackemann b Alderman	0
D.R. Pringle run out	0
†S.J. Rhodes not out	1
Extras (lb 14, w 2)	16
Total (for 7 wkts, 55 overs)	**278**

J.E. Emburey and N.A. Foster did not bat

Fall of wickets: 1-123, 2-180, 3-182, 4-239, 5-266, 6-266, 7-268

Bowling: Alderman 11-2-36-3; Rackemann 11-0-56-1; Lawson 11-0-48-0; Waugh 11-0-70-0; May 6-0-33-0; Moody 5-0-21-1

AUSTRALIA

G.R. Marsh not out	111
D.C. Boon lbw b Foster	19
D.M. Jones c Gower b Emburey	27
*A.R. Border b Pringle	53
S.R. Waugh c Gooch b Foster	35
T.M. Moody not out	6
Extras (lb 18, w 9, nb 1)	28
Total (for 4 wkts, 54.3 overs)	**279**

†M.R.J. Veletta, T.B.A. May, G.F. Lawson, C.G. Rackemann and T.M. Alderman did not bat

Fall of wickets: 1-24, 2-84, 3-197, 4-268

Bowling: DeFreitas 11-1-50-0; Foster 11-0-57-2; Botham 11-0-43-0; Pringle 10.3-0-50-1; Emburey 11-0-61-1

Umpires: B.J. Meyer and D.R. Shepherd

Man of the match: G.R. Marsh

Men of the series: S.R. Waugh (Australia) and G.A. Gooch (England)

Result: Australia won by six wickets

England won series 2-1

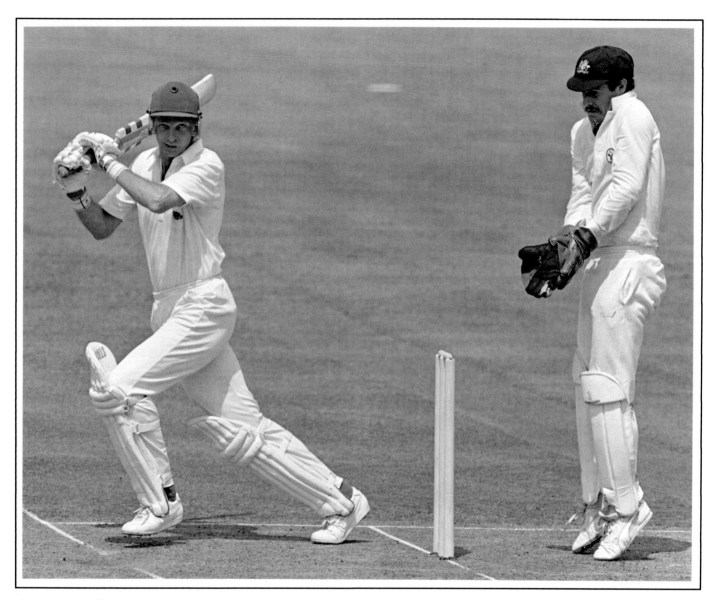

Gower in one of his more elegant moments. He took well to the job of opening the innings, with scores of 36, 28 and 61. Valetta, here keeping wicket, lost his place when the Tests began.

It requires a certain amount of courage, as well as joie de vivre, to turn cartwheels at Lord's with no clothes on, but Sheila Nicholls managed it, apparently on the spur of the moment. The trouble was, she ran off to the Warner stand with her dress on the other side of the ground.

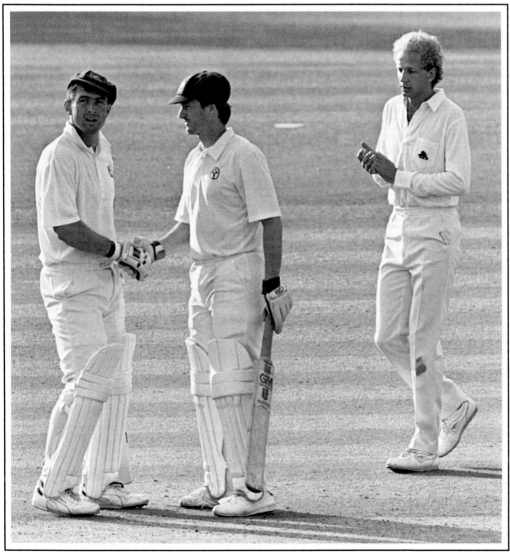

Marsh is congratulated by Waugh after reaching a handsome hundred, his last score of any account for a long while. But his innings took Australia to victory, a feat they achieved in the very last over, with three balls remaining.

A famous victory for

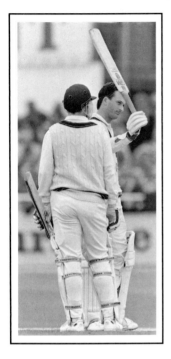

(Above) *Waugh reaches his hundred, his first in Tests.*
(Below) *Headingley before the start of play. Not the most gracious of entrances, but dourly in keeping.*

In the run-up to the first Test nothing went right for the English selectors. Dilley was never going to be ready, but there was no foreseeing that Botham and Gatting would also be ruled out. Botham took a horrible blow from Barwick in a county match, necessitating an operation on his right cheekbone. Gatting, nursing an injured finger, decided he could not hold a bat without discomfort. Robin Smith and Kim Barnett took their places. The Australians had their troubles, too, Rackemann having to undergo an operation on a knee. England finally omitted Emburey. Australia went in without a spinner, too, a grim prospect for the next five days.

The weather had changed, blue skies giving way to low cloud. Gower won his fourth toss in a row and, for reasons never accountable, put Australia in. At the end of the first day they were 207 for 3, showers and bad light having interrupted play. By Friday evening they had reached 580 for 6. From then on England had nothing to play for except a draw, a gloomy proposition at the best of times, but far worse when it was a situation of their own making.

There were soon signs that Gower's gamble was not going to come off. Marsh and Taylor batted for 80 minutes with few moments of unease, the pitch slow and movement in the air negligible. Marsh was lbw to DeFreitas' first ball after lunch, and at 57 Boon, beaten several times by Foster, got a touch to one that left him.

That was more or less the extent of England's success. Border was quick to impose himself, slashing DeFreitas for six over cover and latching on to anything remotely short. He hit nine fours in a stay of just over two hours and not many balls got past the bat. He went once too often for the pull against DeFreitas, the ball flying off the edge to mid-wicket. All this time Taylor, a left-hander of limited range but sound technique, was running quick singles and occasionally driving the over-pitched ball. He should have been out at 89, when Gower dropped him off Foster at third slip, but this apart it was a composed and cool innings, only his fifth in Test cricket.

There was a brief period before lunch when England's bowlers looked awkward, but generally only Foster posed problems. Border, his whiskers removed the day before, got several inside edges and once Newport rapped him on the knuckles. Gooch bowled two overs and they were among the best of the day, on a length and with more swing than anyone else.

Next morning Taylor, 96 not out overnight, batted steadily on. He had begun to bask in the afterglow of a maiden Test hundred, his cover drives now beating the fielders, when he made an impulsive heave at an unsuitable ball from Foster.

Dean Jones, an upright, stylish figure, with something of Dexter's romantic panache, was soon outscored by Waugh. Accepting a secondary role with dignity he

Australia

found himself spectator to a stream of brilliant strokes, mainly off the back foot and savagely struck past cover. The pair had put on 138 when Newport found a good one for Jones. The tendency on the first day had been for the ball to keep low, but this one lifted. Now it was all Waugh, his maiden Test hundred coming off only 124 balls. Chewing relentlessly, he is not an imposing presence but his technique is correct and when he goes for the shot it fairly whistles to the boundary. England's bowling looked monotonous and nondescript, and it was sad to see the initiative squandered so totally and so early.

Waugh reached 150, Healy came and went, and then Hughes saw out the last 90 minutes of the day. Hughes is no beauty at the crease, a stiff and robotic forward stroke played with no back lift his main method of defence. But he had the luck of the devil, edges of varying thickness speeding past the slips. Twice he indulged in huge lunges, the ball flying into the crowd at square leg.

Next morning Border kept England at it while another 21 runs were added. The pitch looked to be playing easily enough but by lunch Gooch had gone for 13, playing outside a good-length ball from Alderman that held its course. There was now some swing for Alderman but Barnett began to play the kind of innings one would have wanted from Gatting. He was quick to get into line and any deviation of length or direction was promptly punished.

Broad had seemed set for the afternoon when Hughes, mischieviously producing a slower ball from the back of the hand, bowled him. Hughes has a short-stepping mincing run-up, rather as if a lobster was nipping at his ankles, but he varied his pace inventively. He bowled unchanged after tea, getting his in-swingers to lift and occasionally putting in a bouncer.

The batting now between Barnett and Lamb was of a quality with that of Jones and Waugh the previous day. Far from suggesting resignation they went at it with grace and purpose. Barnett, scoring even faster than Lamb, hit ten fours in an innings of two-and-a-half hours. He hops around his crease like a demented rabbit but just about in time he settles down and is more or less still when the ball arrives. Essentially a front-foot player, he leaned anything over-

A total about which Gower must have nightmares. Can he ever have seen the like? And last man Hughes 71! Surely the figures are the wrong way round?

But it was, alas, no dream, and Australia were given a gift from the gods. From the start England were on the receiving end and they stayed that way.

(Far left and page 25) Waugh has the typical looks of a certain kind of Australian, slightly pinched features, a no-nonsense expression. As a batsman he has all the attributes, blossoming in the last year to full expression of them. He has no great presence at the wicket, almost a sort of anonymity, but that is to mislead. He walks rather splay-footed, an inelegance that is reassuring.

First Test
Headingley

(Right) Mark Taylor during his innings of 136. He seemed, early on, a batsman with certain limitations, but he produced the shots when necessary and was never ruffled. In view of Marsh's run of failures in the first two Tests, Taylor's growing confidence helped the Australian batsmen all down the order. (Bottom right) He acknowledges applause for his first Test hundred. It would be surprising if there are not a good many to follow. His soundness in defence was no revelation but his driving through the covers showed a new aspect of him.

Gooch (above) is going to bowl and he knows where he wants his fielders. If anything, Gower underbowled him.

pitched to the boundary. Lamb was at his best, hitting the ball on the up and with a fine follow-through. Not out at the end of the day he had hit 19 fours in four hours.

Gower lasted an hour, more charmingly than securely, and it was no great surprise when he glanced languidly at Lawson and was caught by the wicket-keeper. Anxious to get well across to the ball Gower had now become equally vulnerable about the leg stump. Smith kept Lamb company for another hour and with a score of 284 for 4 at the end of the day England had lost nothing in composure or comparison.

In need of 401 to save the follow-on England went along steadily for half an hour. Lamb then was caught off bat and pad at short-leg, Boon just getting down in time. Smith looked full of runs but lunch undid him. Seven balls later he, like Barnett and Gooch before him, and DeFreitas after him, was lbw to Alderman, the pad obstructing the bat. Alderman, bowling from close to the stumps, rarely failed to pitch on a length around off stump, the least movement sufficing to beat the bat.

There was no great trouble in avoiding the follow-on but there was little sting in the

Dean Jones (left). He had not long recovered from a nasty injury to a cheekbone, inflicted by Pigott of Sussex at Hove. But he showed no apprehension against the England pace bowlers, pulling, driving and cutting with his usual panache.

First Test Headingley

(Below) *Mervyn Hughes does not believe in wasting energy by lifting his bat. He drops down on anything suspicious and thumps the others. The ball sometimes flies off in unexpected directions, but the fielders are taken unawares as much as the batsman. (Right) Pringle looks sympathetically at his little friend, but, like his fellow bowlers, he needed something to distract him from the scoreboard.*

(Opposite) *It is no good bowling short to Waugh for he simply makes room and thrashes the ball past cover.*

tail. 171 runs ahead, Australia went in again needing quick runs. They took their time for a while, losing Marsh at 14 and Taylor at 97, Taylor again looking a batsman of quality. Border galvanised Boon into action, and in deteriorating light they went about their business in something of a frenzy. Too much of one for the umpires, who halted play with three overs to go and Border reluctant to leave the field.

Next morning when Border finally declared England were left to score 402 at just under five runs an over or to last something like 83 overs. Broad was soon lbw to Alderman but at lunch, largely by way of sparkling strokeplay from Barnett, England were 66 and the outlook set fair. The pitch was playing as well as at any time in the match, the clouds had rolled away and the sun beat down. Any satisfaction England might have derived from the morning's events, however, was soon dispersed. Barnett, without adding to his score, was caught in two minds playing at Alderman, the ball moving from leg to off and spooning off the bat to slip.

Lamb lasted six balls, caught off bat and pad as in the first innings, only this time Boon had to reach up instead of bend down. Gooch was in no trouble but Gower again waved at anything on his legs, once one-handed and several times just lobbing the ball over or between fielders. Eventually he glanced one and Healy took off to make a fine one-handed catch.

Now England were in real trouble, their prospects not improved when Gooch, who was in a mood to see the match out, was adjudged lbw, after a long stare by the umpire, David Shepherd.

There was no further resistance to speak of. Alderman continually beat the half-prod forward stroke, Hughes and Lawson produced their best bowling of the match, and England went down unheroically.

First Test
Headingley

(Below) Alderman bowls straight and from close to the stumps; any movement, however slight, off the seam, brings trouble. (Right) In his highest Test innings for some time Lamb batted with the same flair and inventiveness that he shows in one-day cricket.

Gower (right) has got this one away all right, but he lived dangerously, both off his legs and outside the off stump. Kim Barnett (far right). His 80 was an exhilarating innings, full of aggression. He is as fidgety as Randall, but head and feet are usually in the right place when the ball arrives.

(Left) Greg Campbell gets
Pringle lbw, his first Test
wicket. Pringle's batting
seemed bereft of the ideas he
often shows in county cricket
and England suffered in
consequence.

First Test Headingley

Border is going well on the Monday evening, too well it seems for the umpires (above) who decided unilaterally that it was no weather for cricket. The rain came in due course but when the players went off there had been scarcely a drop. No wonder he looked aggrieved.

Border does not usually bat one-handed (right) but he probably could against the sort of bowling England served up to him. He had a good match and seemed in ominously fluent form.

Broad (above) is lbw to Alderman for 7, and England are 17 for 1. The touch that brought Broad so many runs in Australia seems temporarily to be missing.

Gower (right) gets everything well away from the ball, so there can be no mistake. He was not always correct in what he chose to play at or to leave alone, but few left-handers are, Border excepted.

First Test Headingley

(Right) Not since the days of Carmody and his umbrella field have the Australian slips looked like this. As Russell faces Hughes all eleven players are in camera range.

(Above) Almost as many slips as for Russell, and Pringle dabs Alderman inelegantly into Border's lap. (Later) Newport does little better, this time Marsh at fourth slip making the catch.

(Below) Healy takes the catch, Russell departs, and Hughes celebrates. For England the situation was one of increasing gloom.

First Test
Headingley

DeFreitas is bowled and it is all over. There could be no excuses for a defeat of such dimensions.

Alderman had the match of a lifetime. He is a bowler without affectations, going about his business unobtrusively and effectively. He bowled few bad balls and hardly any off the wicket. The number of lbw decisions he acquired – quite apart from another dozen that must have been borderline – was evidence of his straightness. He deserved his first ten-wicket haul in a Test, and to be nominated 'Man of the Match'.

The Australians have reason to celebrate. It looks as though Dean Jones, with his clown's painted lips, is using Boon as a ventriloquist's dummy and Steve Waugh seems to be sitting on air; but there was magic in the air.

A decent face on defeat

(Above) *Alderman always appears to have a wolfish grin of anticipation, and well he might have for, in the second innings, without ever departing from the classic virtues of length and direction, he finished with six wickets for 128, nine in the match.*

(Below) *Outside the Grace Gates and a rare fourth-day full house. This is not the most glamorous view of Lord's but, inside, the ground was as pretty as a picture.*

The weather at Lord's remained just about ideal and Gower beat Border in the toss for the fifth time in succession this summer. England had jettisoned Pringle and DeFreitas, while Lamb declared himself unfit. Emburey returned and Dilley and Jarvis came in to share the new ball with Foster. Australia replaced Campbell with the leg-spinner Hohns.

Disinclined to throw away the benefit of batting first a second time, Gower was able to watch his opening pair proceed placidly enough for almost an hour. Then, at 31, Alderman had Broad lbw and what looked like a pitch made for batting showed unsuspected ill-humour.

Hughes, taking over from Alderman, began thumping the ball in just short of a length. Barnett, on view for half an hour in which he hit two boundaries, was picked up at short-leg by Boon and Gatting went the same way first ball. Hughes' figures were now 6-4-5-2, and 31 for 0 had become 58 for 3. It looked likely to be a great deal worse when Gower, on 7, hooked Lawson to Jones at long-leg. Jones does not drop much but he dropped this.

While Gower, as if in gratitude, sprayed boundaries all round the ground, Gooch had the ruminative air of one who intended to be there at the day's end. He was not neglectful of anything short or over-pitched and it was

at last possible to envisage an England score in keeping with the conditions. But such a day-dream was sadly interrupted when Gooch, pushing out at a ball from Waugh that pitched outside the off stump and went away, was caught behind. Smith drove and cut Waugh so fiercely that, despite his taking of Gooch's wicket, he had to be removed after four overs that cost 38 runs.

Again the batting seemed all silk and strength, the bowling being punished at both ends. The partnership had produced 50 in double-quick time when Gower, aiming to cut a ball from Lawson that was both too close to him and of too full a length, chopped it on to his stumps. Emburey was bowled second ball and then Smith, in fine fettle, mishooked Lawson. On a beautiful batting wicket England's spendthrift methods had reduced them to 191 for 7.

On past form the last three hardly looked good for a dozen, but now Russell, so apparently apprehensive at Headingley, showed the benefit of some rewarding net practice against short-pitched deliveries. He batted for nearly three hours, getting resolutely in line and hooking and cover-driving as the bowling demanded. Foster batted almost as well while 46 were scored, reluctantly departing after Jones caught him on the very edge of the square-leg boundary, his impetus in getting there almost making

him cross the rope. Finally England were all out for 286, Australia batting for one over.

England's bowling on the second day was a great improvement on anything produced at Headingley. Marsh again went early and though Taylor and Boon flourished, adding 145 for the second wicket, the game never ran away from England. Every batsman got a fair start and only Border, playing an uncouth sort of sweep against Emburey, could be said to have connived at his dismissal. Boon, dropped in the gully when 53, looked sure of a hundred when he steered Dilley to second slip.

Australia began on Saturday morning at 276 for 6. Only Waugh, 35 not out, remained of the principal batting and if England could keep them to something around 350 there was every prospect of a close finish. In the end, relishing the sun and the bland pitch, Australia made 528. England began untidily, allowing Waugh and Hughes an easy passage, and then Hohns and Lawson were able to continue without ever being ruffled. Gower was widely criticised for using Foster and Jarvis at the wrong ends but the way they bowled it seemed of academic interest. Waugh on-drove and slashed past cover as if continuing his Headingley innings and was left not out with 152. Lawson made 74, his highest Test score, and his stand of 130 with Waugh was a record for the ninth wicket for Australia at Lord's. Jarvis' 31 overs cost 150 for only Healy's wicket, Dilley's 34 overs went for 141 and 2 wickets, Foster's 45 overs for 129 and 3 wickets. Emburey, with 4 for 88 in 42 overs, looked more like a Test match off-spinner than for some seasons.

At the end of a disheartening day England lost three wickets for 58 in the 23 overs left to them. Gooch was lbw in the first over to Alderman, Barnett never suggested a long stay, and at 28 Broad, profiting by Border's attacking field to the extent of several streaky boundaries, lost his off stump to a Lawson ball that came back up the hill.

Some honour was retrieved after the weekend. Gatting was soon gone, playing no stroke yet again to Alderman, but once more Gower and Smith put some flesh on to the skeletal England batting. Gower was dropped in the gully when 26 but this apart, though never seeming as secure as Smith, he played one of his most resolute and engaging innings. He was in for four-and-a-half hours and he hit sixteen fours. Smith hit the same number of boundaries and batted one minute longer. Together they took England from 84 for 4 to 223.

England won the toss

ENGLAND
First Innings
G.A. Gooch c Healy b Waugh	60
B.C. Broad lbw Alderman	18
K.J. Barnett c Boon b Hughes	14
M.W. Gatting c Boon b Hughes	0
★D.I. Gower b Lawson	57
R.A. Smith c Hohns b Lawson	32
J.E. Emburey b Alderman	0
†R.C. Russell not out	64
N.A. Foster c Jones b Hughes	16
P.W. Jarvis c Marsh b Hughes	6
G.R. Dilley c Border b Alderman	7
Extras (lb 9, nb 3)	12
Total (86.5 overs)	**286**

Fall of wickets: 1-31, 2-52, 3-58, 4-131, 5-180, 6-185, 7-191, 8-237, 9-253

Bowling: Alderman 20.5-4-60-3; Lawson 27-8-88-2; Hughes 23-6-71-4; Waugh 9-3-49-1; Hohns 7-3-9-0

AUSTRALIA
First Innings
G.R. Marsh c Russell b Dilley	3
M.A. Taylor lbw b Foster	62
D.C. Boon c Gooch b Dilley	94
★A.R. Border c Smith b Emburey	35
D.M. Jones lbw b Foster	27
S.R. Waugh not out	152
†I.A. Healy c Russell b Jarvis	3
M.G. Hughes c Gooch b Foster	30
T.V. Hohns b Emburey	21
G.F. Lawson c Broad b Emburey	74
T.M. Alderman lbw b Emburey	8
Extras (lb 11, nb 8)	19
Total (158 overs)	**528**

Fall of wickets: 1-6, 2-151, 3-192, 4-221, 5-235, 6-265, 7-331, 8-381, 9-511

Bowling: Dilley 34-3-141-2; Foster 45-7-129-3; Jarvis 31-3-150-1; Emburey 42-12-88-4; Gooch 6-2-9-0

ENGLAND
Second Innings
G.A. Gooch lbw b Alderman	0
B.C. Broad b Lawson	20
K.J. Barnett c Jones b Alderman	3
M.W. Gatting lbw b Alderman	22
★D.I. Gower c Border b Hughes	106
R.A. Smith b Alderman	96
†R.C. Russell c Boon b Lawson	29
J.E. Emburey not out	36
N.A. Foster lbw b Alderman	4
P.W. Jarvis lbw Alderman	5
G.R. Dilley c Boon b Hughes	24
Extras (lb 6, b 6, nb 2)	14
Total (130 overs)	**359**

Fall of wickets: 1-0, 2-18, 3-28, 4-84, 5-223, 6-274, 7-300, 8-304, 9-315

Bowling: Alderman 38-6-128-6; Lawson 39-10-99-2; Hughes 24-8-44-2; Border 9-3-23-0; Hohns 13-6-33-0; Waugh 7-2-20-0

AUSTRALIA
Second Innings
M.A. Taylor c Gooch b Foster	27
G.R. Marsh b Dilley	1
D.C. Boon not out	58
★A.R. Border c sub b Foster	1
D.M. Jones c Russell b Foster	0
S.R. Waugh not out	21
Extras (b 3, lb 4, nb 4)	11
Total (4 wkts 40.2 overs)	**119**

Fall of wickets: 1-9, 2-51, 3-61, 4-67

Bowling: Dilley 10-2-27-1; Foster 18-3-39-3; Emburey 3-0-8-0; Jarvis 9.2-0-38-0

Umpires: H.D. Bird and N.T. Plews
Man of the match: S.R. Waugh
Result: Australia won by six wickets

(Above) *Not the start England wanted to the second innings, but Gooch is out, lbw to Alderman, in the first over without a run scored.*

Second Test
Lord's

(Above, left) Broad is out lbw to Alderman for 18. He turns away, trying to delay the inevitable, but the accusing finger follows him.

Hughes got the decisive wicket, making one rear up at Gower's throat. Gower, not long past his hundred, could only fend it down for Border, close in, to catch. Hughes bowled quite viciously for some overs, treating Smith with real, or possibly considered, enmity. Russell lasted an hour, not often discountenanced, before he was caught off bat and pad, pushing forward.

Smith, four short of his hundred, was bowled by probably the best ball of the day, from Alderman. Pitching around middle-and-off it swung late to take the off stump.

Alderman, having tasted blood, soon removed Foster and Jarvis, both lbw. Surprisingly, Emburey survived the last hour and England, finishing up at 322 for 9, were 80 runs ahead. It was of not much account, unless the predicted storms arrived to help England out. Emburey and Dilley continued for another hour the following morning, leaving Australia to make 118.

Dilley once again quickly removed Marsh and then the storm did come, though from England's point of view it was too short and sweet. Foster, again from the pavilion end, now disposed of criticism that it was the wrong end for him. He had Taylor taken at second slip by Gooch, Border mishooked him to long-leg. Undeterred, Jones went for a similar stroke off his fourth ball, only to sky it for Russell to catch.

Australia were now 67 for 4. Boon and Waugh were having none of this and they made the necessary runs quite comfortably, though Waugh was dropped in the gully by Broad with Australia still 24 short. The match, against all prediction, lasted until the final hour.

England had put a decent face on defeat, but the match belonged, as batsmen, to Boon and Waugh, and to the bowling of Alderman and Hughes.

(Above) Barnett never really looked secure, especially when Hughes dug the ball in. He stabs at this one, and Boon propels himself forward to catch it. England are 52 for 2. (Left) Mike Gatting, in one of the worst patches of his career, is out to Hughes and Boon in similar fashion to Barnett, who can scarcely have got his pads off. In fact it was Gatting's first ball and England were now 58 for 3, Hughes two for 5.

Second Test
Lord's

Gower (right), badly missed at long-leg when he was 7, endeavoured to make up by charm what he lacked in determination. He proceeded mainly by boundaries but this was not a ball to cut and he paid the price, dragging it on to his wicket.

(Opposite, top) Russell may lack Gower's fluency, but his innings of 64 not out did not suffer by comparison in any way. At Headingley he had looked apprehensive, but after some tough net practice against the lifting ball he got well into line here and timed the ball sweetly through the covers.

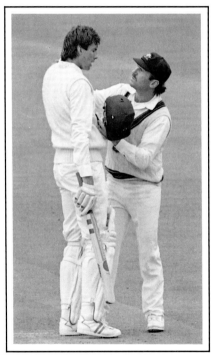

(Above) *Foster, less happily, took one on the helmet and receives sympathy from Border. Foster nevertheless struck some fine blows before he was caught on the very rope edge of the square-leg boundary.*

Second Test
Lord's

(Below, top) The Australian Prime Minister, a useful cricketer himself, watches Australia bat. Bob Hawke narrowly missed a Blue at Oxford. Next to him, on his left, is Allan Border.
(Below) Foster. Gower was strongly criticised for bowling him from the wrong end, but it did not really seem to matter. Foster only came to his best in the second innings, taking three for 39, but the match by then was already lost.

Second Test
Lord's

*The Australian balcony. A
fine show of appreciation for
Steve Waugh's 150.
In defence Waugh (below)
was meticulous almost to the
point of caricature. But
whenever runs were going he
took them, savagely off the
back foot, and smoothly when
driving (opposite). Never
particularly noticeable at the
wicket he piled up the runs as if
in a dream.*

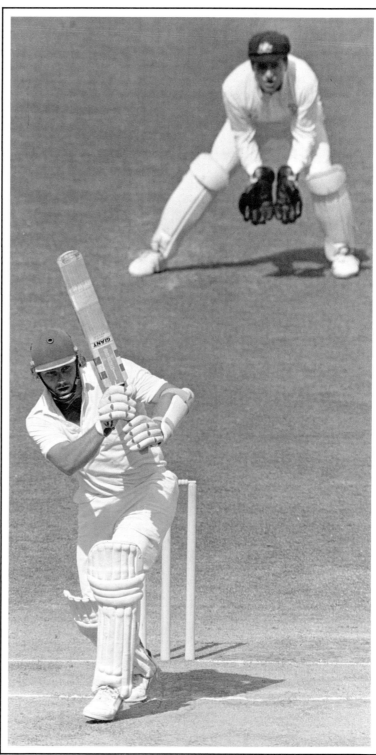

(Above) It looked as though only an exceptional ball would prevent Smith reaching his hundred, but Alderman produced it. He could have waited another over or two, without any harm done.

Far left (top) Lawson does not often stay long, batting as if in a hurry to bowl. But he fancied his chances this time, scarcely ever in trouble. His 74 was his highest Test score, and he put on 130 with Waugh. (Below) Gooch has been turned square by Alderman and the decision was inevitable.

Centre: (left) Robin Smith, with 32 and 96, had a good match, the runs flowing both times he was at the wicket. He plays straighter than most and his driving made the right kind of sound. (Right) Gower answered his critics with a most handsome second-innings hundred. He should have been caught in the gully when he was 26, but he batted all in all for four-and-a-half hours, hitting sixteen boundaries.

Second Test
Lord's

(Above and right) *England on parade, but there was punishment to come. Russell is caught by Boon off Lawson, and now there is little batting left.*

Hughes gets a helping hand from Umpire Plews after flopping on to the pitch, but in truth he needed little help, bowling 28 overs in the heat for only 44 runs.

47

Second Test Lord's

Dilley got rid of Marsh cheaply in each innings, but he was only impressive at odd moments. For the most part he seemed reluctant to put everything in, following injury. This was the only time the quicker English bowlers hit the stumps, the other instance being Emburey's bowling of Hohns.

Left *(above and below) Border hooks Foster and is safely held by the young substitute, Robin Sims, at long-leg. Sims had quite a long wait for it but he judged it like an old hand.*

At 67 for 4, with Jones out to Foster for a duck, Australia may have had an anxious moment or two; but Boon and Waugh wasted no further time. The batsmen (above) help with the stumps, which perhaps may finish up in an Australian back garden. Australia are home by six wickets, and England have a long, hard road ahead.

A match England could

At one moment England looked as if they would be hard put to it to field a side of any sort. For a variety of reasons Foster, Lamb, and Robin Smith declared themselves unfit, and Gatting had to cry off at the last minute when his mother-in-law died suddenly. Fraser replaced Foster and Curtis and Tavaré came in for Lamb and Smith. Botham was to bat at no. 6.

Border for once won the toss and Marsh and Taylor gave Australia their best start so far. Hitherto they had made 44, 14, 6, and 9, but now they went to 88 with scarcely a false stroke.

Emburey was on before lunch and shortly after it he spun one past the advancing Taylor and Russell stumped him.

Six runs later Botham, who had been bowling at a gentle medium pace and with some late movement, had Marsh lbw. Border had been on view for only a quarter of an hour when he raised his bat and bent his knees to a ball from Emburey pitching just outside his leg stump. Border presumably thought it was not worth playing at, but it turned in where his knees would have been and bowled him. Border departed thoughtfully.

With Australia now 105 for 3 England had recovered any lost ground. However, Boon and Jones had put together 96 runs with ominous ease before another wicket fell and it did so with no direct help from the bowlers. Jones drove Jarvis hard back and, with Boon backing up, the ball was deflected on to the stumps off Jarvis' fingers. Boon seemed unable to come to terms with what had happened, Jones flinging down his bat in dismay.

Waugh, the incoming batsman, went across to Jones to comfort him, which was something he did not do to the English bowlers. They had put on 31 together when the heavens opened and turned the ground into a lake. Fraser had been the most economical of the bowlers, probing the off stump, and Jarvis the most costly.

There was only late and modest progress on the second day, Australia adding 62 in 13 overs. Fraser bowled both Waugh and Healy, and Jones went past his hundred. Waugh was well beaten, his wicket falling after 13 hours batting in the series so far, his haul for once out being 393 runs.

There was not much more play on the Saturday either, 31 overs producing 97 runs

Cars sometimes have parking problems at Edgbaston but they are not usually required to float home. The storm that halted play on the Thursday evening was of monsoon proportions, of benefit to England in that another heavy defeat was probably averted.

not afford to lose

for the loss of Hughes. Botham took one catch at slip, but dropped an easier one from Hohns, who bats left-handed.

Border did not declare at the weekend score of 391 for 7, but batted his side out. Jones was finally out for a commanding, and elegant, 157, made in five-and-a-half hours spread over four days, and Fraser picked up two more wickets, giving him impressive figures of 33-8-63-4.

The match might now have appeared dead, but England's batsmen have a magical touch with near corpses. They were soon 47 for 3, Gooch, Gower, and Tavaré all out after brief and inconspicuous appearances. Alderman was beating the bat, particularly after lunch, at will, making nominally high-class players look foolish.

Two wickets fell at 75, Curtis' and Barnett's, but luckily Botham was in sober mood and Russell carried on the good work from Lord's. These two put on 96, batting for almost exactly the same length of time, and making 46 and 42 respectively.

Both left at 171, and England at the end of the fourth day still needed 40 to save the follow-on. The Australians had certainly bowled well, but on so good a pitch it was a pretty abject display.

In the event, the follow-on was saved, but only with the last pair together. Border reflected for ten seconds about the possibility of trying to win the match, but decided against it. Instead Taylor, Marsh, Boon and Healy had some gentle practice on a beautiful afternoon, making 158 for the loss of the first two.

This was a match that England could not afford to lose if the series was to maintain any tension. Almost certainly, without such gross intrusion from the weather – 10 hours were lost, all told – they would have contrived to do so.

Australia won the toss
AUSTRALIA
First Innings

G. R. Marsh lbw b Botham	42
M. A. Taylor st Russell b Emburey	43
D. C. Boon run out	38
★A. R. Border b Emburey	8
D. M. Jones c sub b Fraser	157
S. R. Waugh b Fraser	43
†I. A. Healy b Fraser	2
M. G. Hughes c Botham b Dilley	2
T. V. Hohns c Gooch b Dilley	40
G. F. Lawson b Fraser	12
T. M. Alderman not out	0
Extras (lb 20, nb 17)	37
Total (142 overs)	**424**

Fall of wickets: 1-88, 2-94, 3-105, 4-201, 5-272, 6-289, 7-299, 8-391, 9-421
Bowling: Dilley 31-3-123-2; Jarvis 23-4-82-0; Fraser 33-8-63-4; Botham 26-5-75-1; Emburey 29-5-61-2

ENGLAND
First Innings

G. A. Gooch lbw b Lawson	8
T. S. Curtis lbw b Hughes	41
★D. I. Gower lbw b Alderman	8
C. J. Tavaré c Taylor b Alderman	2
K. J. Barnett c Healy b Waugh	10
I. T. Botham b Hughes	46
†R. C. Russell c Taylor b Hohns	42
J. E. Emburey c Boon b Lawson	26
A. R. C. Fraser run out	12
G. R. Dilley not out	11
P. W. Jarvis lbw b Alderman	22
Extras (b 1, lb 2, nb 11)	14
Total (96.3 overs)	**242**

Fall of wickets: 1-17, 2-42, 3-47, 4-75, 5-75, 6-171, 7-171, 8-185, 9-215
Bowling: Alderman 26.3-6-61-3; Lawson 21-4-54-2; Hughes 22-4-68-2; Hohns 16-8-18-1

AUSTRALIA
Second Innings

M. A. Taylor c Botham b Gooch	51
G. R. Marsh b Jarvis	42
D. C. Boon not out	22
†I. A. Healy not out	33
Extras (b 4, lb 4, nb 2)	10
Total (2 wkts, 65 overs)	**158**

Fall of wickets: 1-81, 2-109
Bowling: Dilley 10-4-27-0; Fraser 12-0-29-0; Emburey 20-8-37-0; Jarvis 6-1-20-1; Gooch 14-5-31-1; Curtis 3-0-6-0

Umpires: H.D. Bird and J.W. Holder
Man of the match: D.M. Jones
Result: Draw

A neat rearrangement of figures shows to Australia's advantage. At their respective half-way stages Australia were 272-5, England 75-5; that just about reflects the disparity between the two teams in confidence, achievement and technique.

Dean Jones, with his Man of the Match bottle. For once Waugh was not centre stage, out for a measly 43 against Jones's handsome 157. Jones at no. 5 was a horrible sight for English bowlers, almost as bad as having to cope with Waugh at no. 6.

Third Test
Edgbaston

Here Taylor, in rather undignified fashion, gets under a Dilley bouncer. There was little else undignified about Taylor, whose defensive skills and cover-driving were a regularly reassuring sight for his colleagues on the Australian balcony.

(Right) This was a rare sight, Emburey giving the ball some air and drawing the batsman down the pitch. Taylor was stumped by some distance, Russell's wicket-keeping in this and later matches being unobtrusively neat.

Unfortunately, Emburey did not capitalise on his success, reverting to a lower trajectory and a pair of close fielders, thus denying the batsman any chance of driving. No off-spinner of any quality has bowled like this in the past, and all such encouragement to flight the ball – from commentators like Benaud downwards – fell on deaf ears. Cook in the next Test was an even more dispiriting purveyor of so-called spin.

Emburey's dismissal of Border, bowled behind his legs, was perhaps the most bizarre dismissal of the series. The ball pitched on the leg stump and Border courteously bent his knees to allow it free passage. Curtis grins boyishly, but in truth there was little to grin about, Boon and Jones adding 96 for the next wicket.

Third Test
Edgbaston

Boon after a flourishing May and a somewhat sour start to June, was back in the runs. He was unlucky to be run out here (right) when backing up, by a ricochet but he made 60 in the match without succumbing to any bowler. Jones was the disbelieving culprit, his fierce drive being diverted by the bowler, Jarvis, on to the stumps, with Boon stranded.

(Opposite) If it was Waugh who took the eye in the first two Tests, it was now Jones's turn. A middle order of Border, Jones, Waugh was perhaps as potentially powerful as any Australia have fielded since the days of Bradman. Jones rarely hung about, his figure at the wicket suggestive of grace and strength. Earlier into the stroke than Waugh, he commanded areas on either side of the bowler less frequently reached by his colleagues.

Third Test
Edgbaston

Jones and Waugh were just getting going when the rains came. These cars look as if they are involved in some sort of aquatic dodgems, but in fact they are Birmingham citizens breasting their way home.

They are the lucky ones, for others were marooned in uncomfortably close proximity or got their feet wet.

Next day there was only thirteen overs of play, and really it was astonishing there were that many.

Waugh, at last, is out, after 13 hours at the crease, spread over three matches, and yielding 393 runs. He was beaten fairly and squarely by Fraser, who won't forget his first Test wicket in a hurry. Fraser ended up with 4 for 63 and was the pick of the English bowlers. He bowled well within himself, mostly on or around the off stump. At Old Trafford, later in the month, he looked to be straining after extra pace and his length suffered in consequence.

Third Test
Edgbaston

Lawson struck the first blow when England batted, Gooch being turned round and adjudged lbw for only 8. Alderman and Hughes reduced England to 75 for 4, and at the same score Waugh had Barnett caught behind the wicket. Waugh was usually the most expensive of the Australian bowlers, but he got the odd wicket to add to his huge tally of runs.

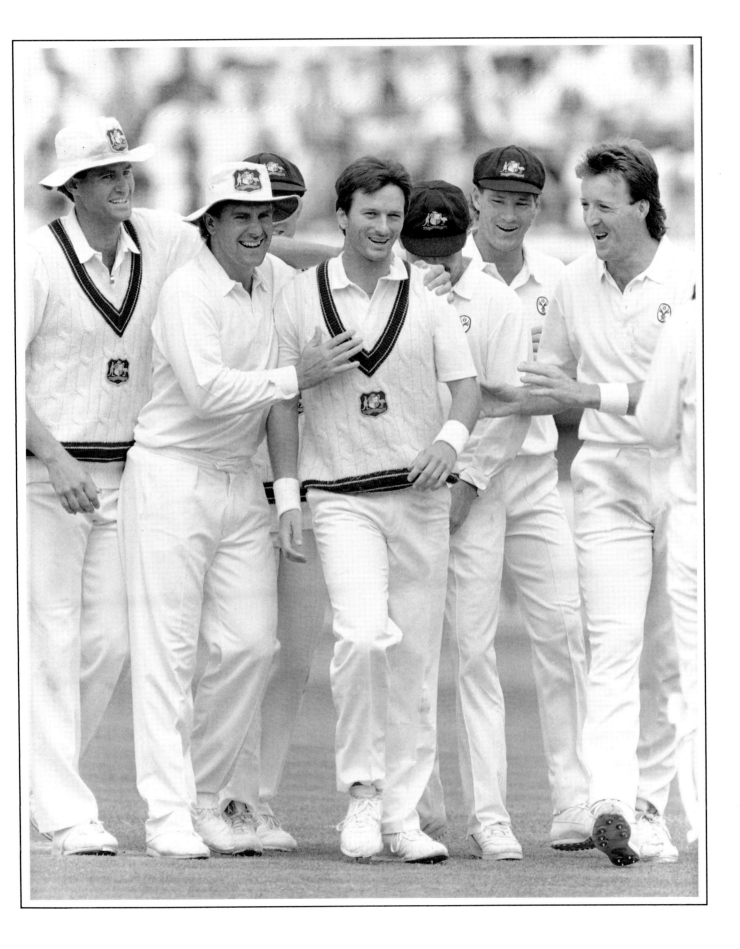

Third Test
Edgbaston

Botham was more circumspect than he often is and in fact his 46 was the modest top score. When he wore a helmet from time to time, it visibly irked him. He never really got under way, unfortunately, and it was not the remembered Botham of old.

Helmeted and visored – on doctor's orders – after his recent fracture of the right cheek, Botham was well and truly bowled by Hughes. The expectations of Botham were perhaps unrealistically great, but his summer of triumphs against the 1981 Australians remains indelible in the memories of all who saw or read about it, and the hope of repeat performances still hung in the air.

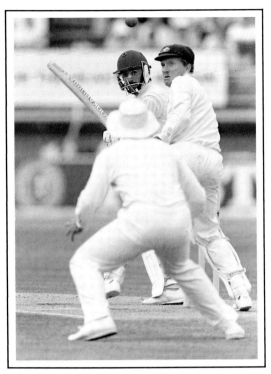

Russell played another useful innings of 46, until he stabbed one from Hohns to slip, via the wicket-keeper. Healy's anxiety turns to joy.

Fraser promised some runs but a misunderstanding with Emburey saw the end of him. All the same, England's last four wickets did rather better than the first four.

Third Test
Edgbaston

Taylor, though he scarcely needed it, gets some gentle batting practice in Australia's second innings, adding 51 to his first innings 43. Border, having no hope of getting a result, decided to bat out the day, rather than give England a chance of losing the match.

Some Australians play straighter than others, but all of them play straighter than England. Here Boon (left) and Healy demonstrate.

At the end of the day, at the end of the match, David Gower has to go through the same old rigmarole. Why didn't England bowl better, bat better? Gower faces the mob and soon runs out of answers. Pilloried in the most ludicrous and disgraceful terms by the tabloids, Gower understandably looked steadily more fed up.

THE TWO CAPTAINS

You would think from the photograph (opposite page) that Allan Border had something to worry about and that David Gower had not a care in the world. But this toss, like nearly everything else, has gone Border's way. How they look merely illustrates the nature of the beast.

The picture was taken at The Oval before the final Test. Border had every reason to be purring, Gower to feel the world was coming to an end, especially if he read the newspapers.

But suppose they had changed places, and Gower had captained the Australians, and Border England? Australia would probably have won the series as easily, England conceivably have put up a better show. Both, in their different ways, played characteristic innings that owed nothing to their press coverage.

Everything seems blurred when Alderman bowls, especially to English batsmen. There is not much rotation of the hips and the arm is not particularly high, but what do such details matter when you can put the ball on a 20p piece, or an inch either way, at will?

(Opposite page) This is characteristic Steve Waugh, a sight repeated ad infinitum through June and July, and one that cover-point must have wearied of.

(Opposite page) Dean Jones was never in trouble in the Tests, but Pigott struck him a horrible blow on his cheek at Hove in May. Far from affecting his confidence, it seems to have done the opposite.

(Above left) Dean Jones in full cry at The Oval, the bat swung high in the follow-through.

(Above right) Hughes seemed intent on getting Smith one way or another, but try as he might he either missed or was clobbered.

(Left) 'Well, it must have been pretty close, I suppose.' Near enough, anyway, to make you want to keep your hat on.

(Opposite page) Gower
batting in lordly fashion at
Lord's, but are the dark socks
forerunners of doom?

Tom Moody (above) scarcely
got a look-in, and here at Trent
Bridge he is run out. But that
is what you expect in one-day
cricket.

Worcester. The circles were cut to confuse, and the Australians, in their first match, duly lost.

(Opposite) *Taylor and Marsh, Trent Bridge, the score 301 for 0 at close of play.*

Old Trafford, fourth Test, and Robin Smith (left) really gets down to it. No one hit harder, on either side.

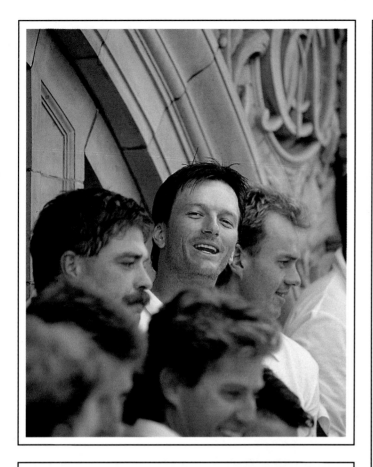

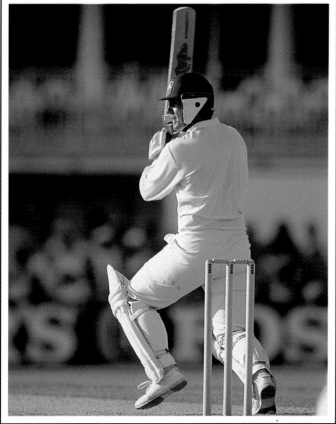

(Top left) Waugh looks happy and so he should. His embryonic beard was the result of the challenges from Boon and Hughes to beat them at their own whiskers.

(Left) Taylor seemed to be batting most of the time, such was his illusion of homeliness. From nowhere, he was suddenly among the highest series scorers of all time. (Above) Now and again Taylor went walkabout to the spinners, this time to Emburey. But never before he, and they, had had enough.

(Top) *The sponsors got their money's worth, all right, though one can't say much for their hats. A few heads at the back are starting to scratch already.* (Left) *It's not much good just looking tough, you've got to act tough. Having made his point, Border got rid of his beard but kept his moustache.* (Above) *Four XXXX's everywhere, but the balloon gives a good view of length, if not of line. When Alderman is bowling, however, if it hits the pad it's probably out.*

(Opposite page) *Watching play at The Oval you get more sense of gas than government. But not far off are the Houses of Parliament, the Thames, and if you look hard enough even a palace or two.*

(Overleaf, right) *Not a dud photograph, but champagne spray in the air. The Ashes get a toasting and whoever drinks the Pol Roger, Four X still has its faithful customers.*

The South African connection

On the final day of the next Test it was announced that a party of sixteen cricketers, under the captaincy of Gatting and managed by David Graveney, the former Gloucestershire captain, would tour South Africa in the New Year. Although rumours of such a tour had long been in the air, no details had emerged hitherto. Besides Gatting, aged 32 and with 68 Test caps, and Graveney, 36, and uncapped, the others were: Athey, Barnett, Broad, Butcher, Christopher Cowdrey, DeFreitas, Dilley, Ellison, Emburey, Foster, French, Jarvis, Maynard and Robinson.

Of these Dilley, Emburey, Barnett, Broad, Jarvis, DeFreitas, Foster and Robinson had appeared for England, in most cases fairly ignominiously, during the current series. It could be said that only DeFreitas, Foster and Jarvis of these had much of a Test future, either through age or proneness to injury of the others. The truly surprising names of those willing to jettison possible careers as England players for unspecified, but undoubtedly considerable sums of money, were Maynard, aged 23 and one Test cap, Jarvis, 24, with six caps, and Foster, 27, with 28 caps. The presence of two black cricketers. Butcher, 36, and DeFreitas, 23, was the most ironical of all. Within a week these two were having second thoughts. Dismayed by the hostile reaction to the tour they withdrew.

Predictably, there was an instant clash between those who saw the players as treacherous mercenaries, either politically naive or downright cynical, and those who sympathised with their wish to save for a comfortable old age. What could scarcely be denied was the disagreeable secrecy and underhand manner of their recruitment.

Such a divisive situation can scarcely have helped towards a happy atmosphere in the England dressing-room. Nevertheless, with the banning of those concerned from Test cricket, the way was now open for something of a fresh look to an England side that had grown old in defeat together.

Whether, in a year's time, those who, for one reason or another, had traded loyalty for money, might regret their decision, was quite another matter. Judging by immediate reactions from South Africa England's simultaneous tour of the Caribbean might prove to be a pleasure cruise in comparison.

Dexter and Gower consult on the square on the Tuesday morning of the Old Trafford Test. Are they studying a batting order or a defectors' list?

England down under

England take the field, defending a modest first-innings total of 260. The heads of the members in the pavilion are turned away from them, as though the arrival of the Australian openers is of more interest.

The toss again went England's way but little else did. There were clouds about and spots of rain when Gooch and Curtis began the innings. These soon dispersed and batting was scarcely affected by the conditions. Lawson, however, was getting a certain amount of swing and inward movement off the seam, enough to bowl Gooch at 23 and get Robinson lbw at the same score. Curtis lasted longer, two hours in fact, but when Lawson bowled him at 57 with a similar delivery he had managed only 22.

The depression surrounding Gower was almost tangible, but, with Robin Smith as companion, he batted as well as at any time in these Tests. Fluently, but without risks, these two took the score to 132 and they looked set for the evening.

Within minutes the innings was in ruins. Hohns had Gower lbw pulling at a shortish ball that kept low, Botham attempted to hit Hohns out of the ground and missed, Russell was lbw to Lawson and then Emburey to Hohns. 132 for 3 had become 158 for 7.

There was some last ditch improvement, with Foster batting jauntily and Smith going to a magnificent hundred. At close of play both were still there: Smith 112, Foster 36. Foster was soon gone next morning, but Smith again batted with dash and authority, his 143 being more than half England's score. He was last out.

The weather, for once, in this torrid July, was miserable, but again the early Australian batsmen thrived. Taylor and Marsh had put together 135, in not the remotest trouble against indifferent bowling, before they were parted. By the end of the day Australia were 219 for 3, with Border digging in and Jones flourishing. For one brief spell, when Marsh, Taylor and Boon went for 19 runs, England's bowlers had a faint sniff of success, but it was soon over. Boon played no stroke at a ball from Fraser that bowled him and Emburey, with one of the few balls that he had flighted, drew Taylor out and had him neatly stumped. Each England bowler proved disappointing in his own particular way, though Botham was allowed only 5 overs, taking 1 for 15, of which 13 came from his first over.

Australia were eventually put out for 447, a mild reprieve for England, since they were 362 for 5 at one stage. Border batted doggedly for 80, over which he took five hours, and Waugh made 92, in 100 minutes less. There was little to be said in favour of the English bowling, Fraser mistakenly pressing for more pace, Foster too often short. Emburey and Cook pursued their own dispiritingly defensive ways, bat-pad catchers squatting near the pitch and the bowlers accommodating them.

When Gooch cuffed Lawson for ten in his first over, it looked as if England might be contemplating something defiant in reply.

Far from it: 10 for 0 became 59 for 6, Lawson and Alderman sharing the wickets. Gooch lasted nearly an hour, managing only 13 before tamely guiding Lawson to first slip; Curtis was out for nought, second ball; caught at short leg; Robinson was lbw after half an hour; Smith was taken down the leg side off his eighth ball, an untidy stroke to a ball that was better left alone.

Alderman was now bowling beautifully and Botham, remorsefully sober, had no answer to his alternating swing. Gower, fatalistically reckless in contrast to his first innings, slashed at Lawson and was caught in the gully.

At 59 for 6 it scarcely seemed to matter whether rain saved England or drowned the whole team. Russell, however, remained unperturbed for over two hours and Emburey kept him good company for the last 80 minutes, a storm emptying the ground at tea-time.

With nine overs of the match left Australia won by 9 wickets, their 100th Test win over England. Their victory was never really in doubt, but for once they were made to fight, Russell and Emburey taking their partnership to 142. They were together at lunch, few balls having got past them. Russell jabbed the short ball off his ribs, often for four, and drove handsomely through the covers. Emburey looked calm and despatched the ball in surprising directions, acquiring ten boundaries.

It took a fine ball from Alderman to bowl Emburey for 64, but by then England had nudged ahead. Foster and Fraser lasted 39 minutes, and Cook 10, but it was not quite long enough to make Border sweat. Russell, so frail in appearance that he looks as if an unexpected gust could carry him off, was left 128 not out, having hit fourteen boundaries, and batted all told just under six hours. It was a performance by a no. 7, in relation to the rest of England's innings, that has had few equals.

Australia required only 78, and they had 70 minutes, plus 20 overs, to make them. They spun it out politely, and could probably have scored twice as many if they had been asked to.

Once more Australia had been on top from the very start of the match and they had played their now customary sound and aggressive cricket. But in terms of newspaper treatment the edge was taken off Russell's splendid innings by the coincidental announcement of the team of English cricketers to tour South Africa.

England won the toss
ENGLAND
First Innings
G.A. Gooch b Lawson	11
T.S. Curtis b Lawson	22
R.T. Robinson lbw b Lawson	0
R.A. Smith c Hohns b Hughes	143
*D.I. Gower lbw b Hohns	35
I.T. Botham b Hohns	0
†R.C. Russell lbw b Lawson	1
J.E. Emburey lbw b Hohns	5
N.A. Foster c Border b Lawson	39
A.R.C. Fraser lbw b Lawson	2
N.G.B. Cook not out	0
Extras (lb 2)	2
Total (130 overs)	**260**

Fall of wickets: 1-23, 2-23, 3-57, 4-132, 5-140, 6-147, 7-158, 8-232, 9-252
Bowling: Alderman 25-13-49-0; Lawson 33-11-72-6; Hughes 17-6-55-1; Hohns 22-7-59-3; Waugh 6-1-23-0

AUSTRALIA
First Innings
M.A. Taylor st Russell b Emburey	85
G.R. Marsh c Russell b Botham	47
D.C. Boon b Fraser	12
*A.R. Border c Russell b Foster	80
D.M. Jones b Botham	69
S.R. Waugh c Curtis b Fraser	92
†I.A. Healy lbw b Foster	0
T.V. Hohns c Gower b Cook	17
M.G. Hughes b Cook	3
G.F. Lawson b Fraser	17
T.M. Alderman not out	6
Extras (b 5, lb 7, w 1, nb 6)	19
Total (167.5 overs)	**447**

Fall of wickets: 1-135, 2-143, 3-154, 4-274, 5-362, 6-362, 7-413, 8-423, 9-423
Bowling: Foster 34-12-74-2; Fraser 36.5-4-85-3; Emburey 45-9-118-1; Cook 28-6-85-2; Botham 24-6-63-2

ENGLAND
Second Innings
G.A. Gooch c Alderman b Lawson	13
T.S. Curtis c Boon b Alderman	0
R.T. Robinson lbw b Lawson	12
R.A. Smith c Healy b Alderman	1
*D.I. Gower c Marsh b Lawson	15
I.T. Botham lbw b Alderman	4
†R.C. Russell not out	128
J.E. Emburey b Alderman	64
N.A. Foster b Alderman	6
A.R.C. Fraser lbw b Hohns	3
N.G.B. Cook c Healy b Hughes	5
Extras (lb 6, w 2, nb 5)	13
Total	**264**

Fall of wickets: 1-10, 2-25, 3-27, 4-28, 5-38, 6-59, 7-201, 8-223, 9-255
Bowling: Lawson 31-8-81-3; Alderman 27-7-66-5; Hohns 26-15-37-1; Hughes 14.4-2-45-1; Border 8-2-12-0; Waugh 4-0-17-0

AUSTRALIA
Second Innings
G.R. Marsh c Robinson b Emburey	31
M.A. Taylor not out	37
D.C. Boon not out	10
Extras (nb 3)	3
Total (1 wkt)	**81**

Fall of wicket: 1-62
Bowling: Foster 5-2-5-0; Fraser 10-0-28-0; Emburey 13-3-30-1; Cook 4.5-0-18-0

Umpires: B.J. Meyer and J.H. Hampshire
Man of the match: G.F. Lawson
Result: Australia won by nine wickets

There is a certain neatness about the figures on the scoreboard, no. 5, Robin Smith, having made exactly half the total. By the time the innings ended, he had contributed considerably over half. Time and again, when it was too late to be relevant, the runs scored by England's lower-order batsmen, exceeded those made by their seniors. In this match England's seventh first-innings wicket fell at 158, the remaining three adding 102. In the second innings England were 59 for 6, the last four wickets putting on 205.

Fourth Test
Old Trafford

Gooch had a bad match, Lawson getting him in both innings for 11 and 13. Gooch was unhappy about his form and offered to stand down to give someone else a chance in the next Test. There was no real rival to Gooch as an opening batsman, but it was true he was not batting in the commanding manner one associates with him. Too often Alderman found him with pad obstructing bat, and in this match Lawson first bowled him and then had him caught off a weak stroke at slip.

(Opposite) Three English wickets went down for 57, all of them to Lawson, whose bowling steadily improved as the series went on. He looks youthful enough here, congratulated by his team-mates, and as he settled into a more comfortable rhythm, so did his stride take on a new elasticity and vigour. He took nine wickets in this Test, and was named Man of the Match.

Fourth Test
Old Trafford

(Left) Smith seems to have recognised an old friend in the stands, but Gower isn't sure whether it's a cobber with a Foster's or a pretty girl he is pointing at. While these two were going well together a decent score was on the cards, but 130 for 3 was soon 158 for 7. (Below) This was rock bottom for Botham, bowled by Hohns for 0, taking an almighty swing and missing. In the second innings he batted soberly for 4.

(Opposite page) Smith played many fine strokes, all of them with conviction. He defended in the same positive manner. His square-cutting stung the hands of whoever got in the way and his driving was beyond the fielders' chasing.

Fourth Test
Old Trafford

(Right) *The batsman at the bowler's end is so far out of his ground that, if Lawson deflected Smith's drive, he must surely have been given out. He was not, however, so there must be some other explanation.*

(Below) *Robin Smith, last out for 143, gets generous applause, from the Australians as well as from the members. Here, at last, was an English batsman who had come to stay, via South Africa and Hampshire, where the great Barry Richards had preceded him.*

Marsh is neatly caught on the
leg side by Russell standing up
to Botham. Botham was rather
under-bowled for once, being
allowed only five overs during
the day. He had 13 taken off
his first over, the remaining
four costing only 2.

Russell's wicket-keeping
was as usual unobtrusive and
impeccable, his judgement of
line requiring no late scuffle to
get into position. There is
something Peter Sellers-like
about this appeal, but when
Russell asked they were
usually out.

Fourth Test
Old Trafford

(*Above*) *Border during his innings of 80. He may have left the heavy scoring to others but his own various innings, though undemonstrative, were exactly what was required. Not out almost more often than out, he had a healthy average to show for his patience.*

(*Right*) *Marsh's wicket was usually the first Australian one to fall, but on occasions he could certainly make Gower jump to it. Waugh (opposite, top) for once made less than a hundred, but only eight less. Border (opposite, below) looks anxious but this was no catch. (Far right) Gower and Botham had not seen each other apparently for some time. So Gower comments on Botham's weight loss while Botham says Gower has grown. It is not the beginning of a new dance.*

Fourth Test
Old Trafford

(Right) *Not* again, *says Curtis, but alas it is; and Boon, half-hidden, has caught him second ball at short-leg off Alderman. Botham too (below) knows the worst and Alderman claims his third wicket in the second innings.*

(Above, left) *Smith, playing a rare, untidy stroke to a ball well wide of the leg stump, is caught by Healy. This area was Smith's one real weakness, his head tending to fall away and so unbalance him. (Above, right) Gooch is out cheaply for the second time, dabbing a gentle catch to Alderman at slip, off Lawson. Not often is Gooch out to so half-hearted a stroke. (Below) Gower on the lonely walk back after being well caught by Marsh in the gully off*

Lawson for 15. It was yet another instinctive twitch of a stroke, made without thought of the consequence. Australians never got themselves out in this reckless fashion.

All of Jack Russell's determination and correctness is in this defensive stroke, bat and pad the nearest of neighbours. Although Russell's fragility might appear to be against him, his timing made up for any lack of brute strength.

(Above)Border shakes Russell by the hand after he reaches his maiden hundred, an innings of extraordinary composure, which unfortunately merely delayed the inevitable for England. Australia needed only 78 to win, and Taylor (right), though scarcely out of form, helped himself to some gentle practice and another 37 runs.

Fourth Test
Old Trafford

*It's all over, the series and the
Ashes gone to the vastly better
organised and more technically
correct team. Umpire Meyer
doffs his cap, Emburey collects
a stump after his last
appearance for England, and
Boon and Taylor receive
handshakes. On a gentle sunlit
evening the shadows grow
large on the field, the end of a
long road for some, the dawn of
a new era for others.*

(Left) To the victors, the spoils, and Allan Border, not given to gratuitous smiling, shares his pleasure with his star batsman and bowler, and his comfortable opening pair. (Replica of the Ashes reproduced by courtesy of David Frith.)

But for Dexter, Gower and Stewart (below) there are the probing questions and the tiresome necessity of providing answers where there really aren't any. Nobody bargained for so one-sided a series, for so suddenly formidable an Australian side, so depressingly ill-equipped an English one. Let alone the South African intervention.

Australia on top again

One of the main differences between the two teams was that, whereas England's batsmen, especially in the early part of the innings, always looked like getting out, the Australians hardly ever did. Marsh had hitherto been the sole excepton, but this time he put that right with a vengeance. At the end of a thankless first day for England's bowlers he was 125 not out, Taylor, his prolific partner, 141 not out. With the help of 35 extras, including 19 no-balls, Australia, despite a slow outfield, reached 301 for 0 in the last over of the day. This was the first time that a pair of batsmen had batted out the day in a Test in England, the ninth time altogether in Test history. Marsh was within a whisker of being lbw to Devon Malcolm in the fourth over and Taylor was put down at slip early on, but that was about it. The pitch was easy-paced and, once they had settled in, there was an inevitability about the Australian batting. Both Marsh and Taylor reached their highest scores in Tests, and throughout the day they accumulated runs at a steady three per over. England have bowled much less well with more reward, but Taylor and Marsh are percentage players, and when they are on to a good thing they stick to familiar avenues for their runs. England fielded quite decently, Gower being outstanding on both sides of the wicket.

So, for the fifth time in succession, England were in an inferior position, with nothing but respectability to seek, at the end of the first day.

By the time Marsh and Taylor were parted, at 329, they had shared in the highest opening stand in the history of England-Australia Tests. Cook, bowling slower and giving the ball more air, broke the partnership after it had been in operation for more than seven hours, Marsh rather wearily mistiming a heave. Cook's next victim, 101 runs later, was Taylor, more authentically lured out and stumped for 219. Boon went to work with relish and had made 73 before he went the same way. In between whiles he revealed Hemmings' fallibility as a catcher and put the unlucky Botham more or less out of the match, Botham dislocating a finger in trying to catch him off Malcolm.

Jones as usual looked impressive but was out to Fraser for 22. Most curious of all Waugh, clipping a legside half-volley from Malcolm, was picked up by Gower at square-leg without scoring. Malcolm had more than deserved his first Test wicket, having given most of the batsmen uncomfortable moments, and looked decidedly quick. He bowled some useful bouncers and ended the day with an accidental beamer to Border, earning a look of displeasure from the Australian captain. Unfortunately his one wicket had already cost 141 runs.

Border did not keep England at it for long on the Saturday morning, declaring at 602 for 6, with his own score 65. Even on so bland a pitch one expected England to contrive difficulties and there was not long to wait.

Trent Bridge (below) has almost as bleak and unimposing an entrance as Headingley, but it has history, atmosphere and a certain serenity. Whatever others may think about it, Mark Taylor and Geoffrey Marsh can only have the happiest of memories. Alderman and Robin Smith, too.

With the score on 1, Moxon pushed tentatively out at Alderman and Waugh scooped him up at second slip. Atherton thrust his pad out at his second ball but failed to get his bat to it. That was 1 for 2, in the first over. At 14 Curtis, going back, was late on one that kept low from Alderman, his situation not helped by his bat coming down in a hideous line from gully to mid-wicket.

Gower survived until lunch, but departed ingloriously soon afterwards, Healy making a straightforward catch at the second attempt. Lawson was now looking every bit as dangerous as Alderman, making the ball dart away as well as cut back.

Once these two were rested, the game changed, for Hughes came on and Smith launched a devastating attack on him, taking 30 runs off three overs. The afternoon in fact was made glorious by Smith's assault on each bowler in turn, his square-cutting and savage driving a sight for sore eyes. This was an innings of comparable ferocity and spirit to Dexter's 70 against the West Indies pace attack on a dark day at Lord's more than twenty-five years ago.

Russell kept Smith company in his now expected pert and unhustled fashion while 82 were added. Smith went on to a dazzling hundred, and then, as sometimes happens, was out immediately afterwards to a non-descript ball from Alderman that he went to cut. Most of his runs had come from similar shots, so it was not a stroke to criticise.

Hemmings had some fun now, biffing and ballooning the ball away, and encouraging Fraser. Rather too cocky, Hemmings eventually dragged Alderman on to his stumps and Fraser, after playing the quicker bowlers adequately, made nothing of Hohns' leg-spin. Botham, batting with one hand more or less, defended bravely, but he, too, went before the end, England finishing at 246 for 9.

If England's second innings began not quite so disastrously as their first, there was little in it. Gower, changing places with Moxon for no very discernible reason, was bowled by Lawson for 5, padding up. Curtis was again lbw to Alderman, this time on the front foot but with bat equally adrift.

There was hope of partial reprieve during the hour Atherton and Smith were together, Smith not quite in the demolishing mood of the first innings but going well enough until Hughes bowled him with a ball that hit the base of the stumps on the full.

With Botham unable to bat, it was now speedily downhill all the way. Moxon was

AUSTRALIA
First Innings

G.R. Marsh c Botham b Cook		138
M.A. Taylor st Russell b Cook		219
D.C. Boon st Russell b Cook		73
*A.R. Border not out		65
D.M. Jones c Gower b Fraser		22
S.R. Waugh c Gower b Malcolm		0
†I.A. Healy b Fraser		5
T.V. Hohns not out		19
Extras (b 6, lb 23, w 3, nb 29)		61
Total (6 wkts dec. 206.3 overs)		**602**

M.G. Hughes, G.F. Lawson and T.M. Alderman did not bat.
Fall of wickets: 1-329, 2-430, 3-502, 4-543, 5-553, 6-560
Bowling: Fraser 52.3-18-108-2; Malcolm 44-2-166-1; Botham 30-4-103-0; Hemmings 33-9-81-0; Cook 40-10-91-3; Atherton 7-0-24-0.

ENGLAND
First Innings

T.S. Curtis lbw b Alderman		2
M.D. Moxon c Waugh b Alderman		0
M.A. Atherton lbw b Alderman		0
R.A. Smith c Healy b Alderman		101
*D.I. Gower c Healy b Lawson		11
†R.C. Russell c Healy b Lawson		20
E.E. Hemmings b Alderman		38
A.R.C. Fraser b Hohns		29
I.T. Botham c Waugh b Hohns		12
N.G.B. Cook not out		2
D.E. Malcolm c Healy b Hughes		9
Extras (lb 18, nb 13)		31
Total (76.5 overs)		**255**

Fall of wickets: 1-1, 2-1, 3-14, 4-37, 5-119, 6-172, 7-214, 8-243, 9-244
Bowling: Alderman 19-2-69-5; Lawson 21-5-57-2; Hohns 18-8-48-2; Hughes 7.5-0-40-1; Waugh 11-4-23-0

Second Innings

*D.I. Gower b Lawson		5
T.S. Curtis lbw b Alderman		6
M.A. Atherton c and b Hohns		47
R.A. Smith b Hughes		26
M.D. Moxon b Alderman		18
†R.C. Russell b Lawson		1
E.E Hemmings lbw Hughes		35
A.R.C. Fraser b Hohns		1
N.G.B. Cook not out		7
D.E. Malcolm b Hughes		5
I.T. Botham absent injured		—
Extras (b 3, lb 6, w 1, nb 6)		16
Total (55.3 overs)		**167**

Fall of wickets: 1-5, 2-13, 3-67, 4-106, 5-114, 6-120, 7-134, 8-160, 9-167
Bowling: Alderman 16-6-32-2; Lawson 15-3-51-2; Hughes 12.3-3-1-46-3; Hohns 12-3-29-2

Umpires: D.R. Shepherd and N.T. Plews
Man of the match: M.A. Taylor.
Result: Australia won by an innings and 180 runs

The end of a perfect day, and there was more to come next morning. To Gower and his bowlers these figures belonged to nightmare, with not a redeeming feature. When it was England's turn they changed rapidly to 37 for 4, with all but Robin Smith of the main batsmen gone.

Fifth Test
Trent Bridge

Geoff Marsh (above) was not extravagant in his driving but when he timed it right it travelled. This picture looks like a 'Spot the Ball' competition, but Smith knew where it went all right.

(Right) The Trent Bridge pavilion has not much architectural unity about it, but unlike Lord's no ties or jackets are necessary, and women are actually encouraged, outside anyway.

(Opposite page) Taylor never looked other than solid and phlegmatic. He is comfortably built, always had his sleeves rolled down, and kept helmet and visor on, though never in the remotest danger of being hit. He provided Border with a first course of uninterrupted lavishness.

bowled between bat and pad by Alderman and Russell was beaten by a beauty from Lawson. Atherton made a number of crisp strokes through and into the covers and was just beginning to look the part when Hohns held on to a low, hard-driven return catch.

Fraser again was in a total fog against Hohns, but the dying minutes were enlivened by some cheerful hitting from Hemmings. The Australians seemed to get rather less fun out of it, a slip catch claimed by Waugh off Lawson being disregarded by Hemmings and then by the umpires. This led to some unpleasant exchanges, but since Australia were comfortably home by an innings and plenty with a day to spare, there was not really much to complain about. Once again the two opening bowlers had cleared the way and Hohns and Hughes had polished the innings off.

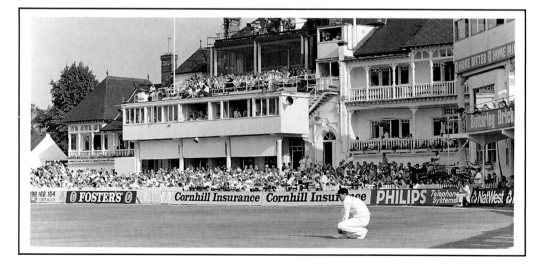

Fifth Test
Trent Bridge

(Right) *Almost unrecognisable without his helmet and visor, Taylor acknowledges the cheers on one of the milestones to his 219. His bat, 'made of English willow', carries a strange animal as its emblem, but it always made the right noises and runs poured forth from it seemingly without effort.*
(Opposite page, top left) *Helmets make for hot heads and now and again fluids have to be replaced. Australia's drink waiters had to be content with their job, for Australia used only twelve men in the whole series, and no matter how well the others played they had little chance of replacing anyone. In contrast to England's dreadful record of injury the Australians were always match fit, with only Rackemann being ruled out early on.*

(Above, right) *301 and still going strong;* (left, below) *but it seems a pity to water the flowers instead of drinking the stuff.*

Fifth Test
Trent Bridge

Allan Border (above) made no hundreds, but even batting well within himself managed to get into the fifties and sixties in almost every match. Once upon a time he bore the burden of Australia's batting, so the present situation must seem a luxury.

(Right) Waugh returns looking rather crestfallen after making 0. He should worry, with the score 553 for 5 and his own average still about 100! Nevertheless, he seemed to have gone slightly off the boil in August. On the other hand Boon (far right) returned to the robust form he had shown in May.

Alderman's first over. Moxon (left) is scooped up by Waugh at second slip, and England are 1 for 1. Atherton (below, left) failed to get his bat in front of his pad, which made it 1 for 2. Altogether Alderman (below), with 5 for 69 and 2 for 32, was always a pleasure to watch. He is not obviously athletic, with his relaxed, shuffling, slightly flat-footed approach and round shoulders, but his arm is high enough and his variations of pace, line and movement, on a perfect length, lethal.

Fifth Test
Trent Bridge

Curtis (right) is lbw on the back foot, the ball keeping a shade low but the bat horribly across the line. Gower (below) had a thoroughly undistinguished match, making 11 and 5. Here Healy grabs a straightforward catch at the second attempt, off Lawson.

Only Robin Smith, in innings after innings, took the fight to the Australians. He cut and drove with immense power, but, even more importantly, exuded the kind of confidence otherwise so lacking.

Fifth Test
Trent Bridge

In the second innings Gower, choosing to go in first, left a ball from Lawson which cut back at him. The means of his getting out were distressingly similar, but there was never reason to suppose Gower was taking it lightly. He simply seemed doomed, though even in his darkest moments (right) he was able to smile, if rather ruefully.

Fifth Test
Trent Bridge

Atherton (above), on a pair, batted with crisp assurance in his second innings of 47. He began as if out of his depth but grew visibly in confidence. He was out when Hohns held a fierce return catch, just as he was coming into his own.

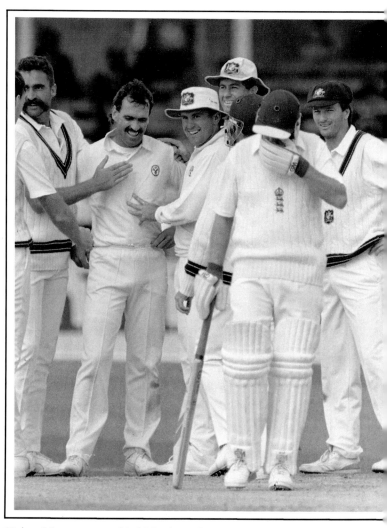

Hohns (above, second left) basks in the applause, Hemmings weeps. But Hemmings had some tricks up his sleeve to display, with jolly innings of 38 and 35. Hohns did not get a great deal of bowling, but usually took a wicket or two when it was needed. He also showed up a woeful lack of technique by England's lower-order batsmen, when confronted by leg-spin.

Devon Malcolm (left) goes through with his drive but the ball has hit the stumps. He did hit a six, bowled fast, and took a wicket. Unfairly, it cost 166 runs.

Boon (below) leads the singing of 'Australia you XXXX beauty', a dressing-room ritual calculated to celebrate victory and banish homesickness at one and the same time.

Australia in easy command

Men of the Series, Jack Russell and Terry Alderman. There could be little dispute about their respective worthiness, though Robin Smith must have run Russell close, and Taylor, Jones and Waugh short-heads behind Alderman.

For the sixth time in succession injuries took heavy toll of the team England had hoped to field. Fraser, DeFreitas and Botham were declared unfit at varying stages and of those finally able to make it to The Oval, Hussain, a newcomer from Essex, and Hemmings were left out. Small, Igglesden, Pringle and Capel were to form the job-lot attack, chosen *faute de mieux* rather than as intended selections, with Cook as the solitary spinner.

Border won the toss and took first use of the best Test batting wicket, as last year, of the summer. This time Taylor and Marsh did not bat out the day, their manner of batting and that of Boon who followed them suggesting that enough was enough. Marsh mishooked Small at 48, and Taylor followed a widish one from Igglesden at 130. Boon was in a boisterous mood, cutting and driving his way to 46, before slicing Small to third slip.

149 for 3 was, by the Australian standards of this summer, a near collapse but Border soon made it plain there were going to be no easy pickings while he was around. By the end of the day he had batted nearly 3½ hours for 66, few balls getting past his bat. At the other end Jones, reassured that his captain meant business, was enabled to play with his usual savage assurance. He hit sixteen boundaries, a high proportion of them back into the bowler's territory, and his 114 took only two hours and forty-two minutes. Small, once he had satisfied himself that he, too, was not going to break down, was lively on occasion, but there was little threat from the others on so docile a pitch.

With Border and Jones still there overnight, there seemed every prospect of 325-3 being doubled by evening. But both these two went early, Border to a mistimed pull at Capel's first ball, and Jones to a fantastic one-handed slip catch by Gower off Small. Only Healy and Hohns of the others stayed for any length of time, a curiously out-of-sorts Waugh playing Igglesden on to his stumps. Pringle took the last four wickets, some compensation for unrewarded bowling earlier in the season.

So, in dreadful light and with rain in the offing, Gooch and Stephenson set out to see what they could knock off the 269 England needed to save the follow-on. There was time for only ten balls to be bowled before rain set in, but these were enough for Gooch, who was possibly unlucky to be given out lbw to the third, having let two pronounced out-swingers go harmlessly by.

The third day, the Saturday, was fitfully

wet and unpleasant but in the three hours play possible, England went the familiar route, reaching only 124 for 6. Alderman and Lawson again bowled beautifully, and Hughes with enough malice to be officially warned for hurling down three successive bouncers at Smith. Atherton and Stephenson both promised briefly, Atherton finally edging an airy off-drive and Stephenson, having taken a nasty knock on the hand from Hughes, was out next ball to Alderman.

Smith threatened until Lawson made a mess of his stumps with an in-swinger that found him rooted to the crease. Alderman was altogether too various for Capel and Russell, and this time it was Gower who quietly held what was left of the innings together.

The week-end seemed to have had a calming effect, for Gower batted so elegantly and with such perfect timing for a while – his defensive strokes for once as instinctively correct as his pulling and driving – that it seemed inconceivable he would not make a hundred or more. No-one on either side in the whole series played with such mastery and with so light a touch as Gower did on this fourth morning, but, then, just as a large crowd was settling happily in appreciation, it was all over, in the usual dispiriting fashion. Alderman pitched a ball of full length outside his leg stump and Gower flicked it on its way to Healy.

England were not so easily done this time, however, Pringle, secure enough until undone by Hohns' leg-spin, and Cook keeping Gladstone Small company while the latter despatched the quicker bowlers with the flourish of one who had been picked for his batting. Small reached his fifty, the follow-on was saved – an unlikely prospect at 98 for 6 – and yet again the tail had made nonsense of what had gone before. England were all out for 285, and Alderman had picked up five wickets yet again.

Australia, though losing Marsh for 4, found no difficulties in the pitch, Taylor and Boon boosting an already formidable lead. Border and Jones carried on the same way, Border warily, Jones with profligate exuberance. A declaration seemed in order around 12.15 with a lead of about 350, but Border carried on until lunch, himself reaching yet another unbeaten fifty.

It seemed an odd decision, but going by precedent Border might be forgiven for assuming that two periods of play would be

Australia won the toss
AUSTRALIA
First Innings

G. R. Marsh c Igglesden b Small		17
M. A. Taylor c Russell b Igglesden		71
D. C. Boon c Atherton b Small		46
★A. R. Border c Russell b Capel		76
D. M. Jones c Gower b Small		122
S. R. Waugh b Igglesden		14
†I. A. Healy c Russell b Pringle		44
T. V. Hohns c Russell b Pringle		30
M. G. Hughes lbw b Pringle		21
G. F. Lawson b Pringle		2
T. M. Alderman not out		6
Extras (b 1, lb 9, nb 9)		19
Total (132.3 overs)		**468**

Fall of wickets: 1-48., 2-130, 3-149, 4-345, 5-347, 6-386, 7-409, 8-447, 9-453

Bowling: Small 40-8-141-3; Igglesden 24-2-91-2; Pringle 24.3-6-70-4; Capel 16-2-66-1; Cook 25-5-78-0; Atherton 1-0-10-0; Gooch 2-1-2-0

ENGLAND
First Innings

G. A. Gooch lbw b Alderman		0
J. P. Stephenson c Waugh b Alderman		25
M. A. Atherton c Healy b Hughes		12
R. A. Smith b Lawson		11
★D. I. Gower c Healy b Alderman		79
D. J. Capel lbw b Alderman		4
†R. C. Russell c Healy b Alderman		12
D. R. Pringle c Taylor b Hohns		27
G. C. Small c Jones b Lawson		59
N. G. B. Cook c Jones b Lawson		31
A. P. Igglesden not out		2
Extras (b 2, lb 7, w 1, nb 13)		23
Total (92.1 overs)		**285**

Fall of wickets: 1-0, 2-28, 3-47, 4-80, 5-84, 6-98, 7-169, 8-201, 9-274

Bowling: Alderman 27-7-66-5; Lawson 29.1-9-85-3; Hughes 23-3-84-1; Hohns 10-1-30-1; Waugh 3-0-11-0

AUSTRALIA
Second Innings

M. A. Taylor c Russell b Small		48
G. R. Marsh lbw b Igglesden		4
D. C. Boon run out		37
★A. R. Border not out		51
D. M. Jones b Capel		50
S. R. Waugh not out		7
Extras (b 2, lb 7, nb 13)		22
Total (4 wkts dec., 63 overs)		**219**

Fall of wickets: 1-7, 2-100, 3-101, 4-189

Bowling: Small 20-4-57-1; Igglesden 13-1-55-1; Capel 8-0-35-1; Pringle 16-0-53-0; Cook 6-2-10-0

ENGLAND
Second Innings

G. A. Gooch c and b Alderman		10
J. P. Stephenson lbw b Alderman		11
M. A. Atherton b Lawson		14
R. A. Smith not out		77
★D. I. Gower c Waugh b Lawson		7
D. J. Capel c Taylor b Hohns		17
†R. C. Russell not out		0
Extras (lb 1, w 1, nb 5)		7
Total (5 wkts, 46.1 overs)		**143**

Fall of wickets: 1-20, 2-27, 3-51, 4-67, 5-138

Bowling: Alderman 13-3-30-2; Lawson 15.1-2-41-2; Hughes 8-2-34-0; Hohns 10-2-37-1

Umpires: H. D. Bird and K. E. Palmer
Man of the match: D. M. Jones
Result: Match drawn
Men of the series: T. M. Alderman (Australia)
R. C. Russell (England)
Result of the series: Australia won the Ashes, 4-0

Geoff Lawson (above), it is good to see, has family ties. His TV message saves the expense of a card, too. Opposite page (below). The Oval, outside the Hobbs Gates. One day, cricket grounds will have to get round to making their entrances more inviting. Some creepers over blank walls, a tree or two, and a few shrubs might help.

Sixth Test
The Oval

Gladstone Small is not always airborne and, to start with at The Oval, he looked to be feeling his back. However once he got going, he really took off.

quite adequate to dispose of England's batsmen.

He was too nearly right for comfort, England losing five wickets for 143 before bad light put a merciful end to proceedings around 5.20 pm. Smith was not out 77, an innings of icy belligerence, played while Alderman, Lawson and Hohns were brushing aside his colleagues, Stephenson for 11, Gooch for 10, Atherton for 14, Gower for 7, Capel for 17. They all bowled well, but on so good a pitch it should not have been as easy as that.

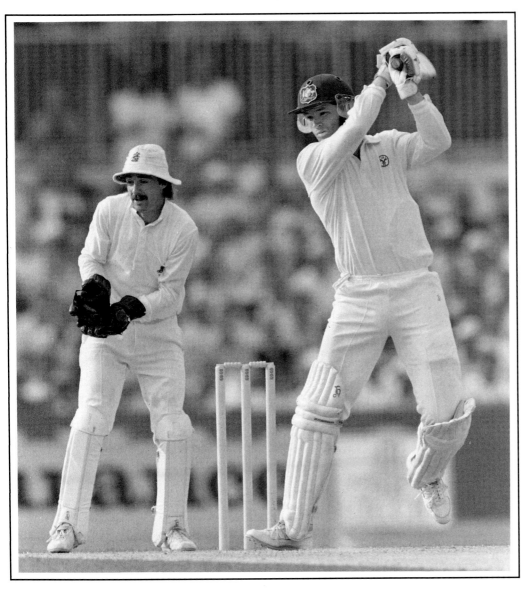

(Left) Dean Jones took his batting light-heartedly. With Border entrenched at the other end he could give full rein to a dazzling array of shots. (Above) He reaches his hundred. One of several adherents to lip salve, he put conservation above aesthetics. Still, it is hard to believe that the English sun, even in this torrid summer, ever did anyone any harm.

Sixth Test
The Oval

Pringle, drafted in as about tenth choice after injuries, abstentions, and defections, cleaned up the last four wickets, in this case getting Hughes lbw. The short-leg's anti-rabies muzzle cannot contribute to serenity. A little more devil in his bowling, and a lot more dash in his batting, and Pringle could progress to being a proper Test all-rounder.

Border (left) never got his century, though he was well on the way several times. Not one to throw his wicket away, Border exemplified all the traditional assets of the Australian cricketer. Healy (above) was one of the few Australians who batted to rather less than his reputation. He sprang to life in this innings, though, striking boundaries all over the place.

Sixth Test
The Oval

Robin Smith (above) seemed to bring real malevolence out of Hughes (right), perhaps because Smith usually despatched him as if he was just a trundler from the outback. Umpire Bird, after three successive bouncers from Hughes to Smith, had words with Border (top right) who seemed not to appreciate it. But what, for God's sake, are umpires for, if not to enforce rules? They do it rarely enough as it is.

(Opposite page) Robin Smith deserves a more flattering picture than this. But Lawson, with a ball of full length that squeezed between bat and pad, really did bowl him neck and crop.

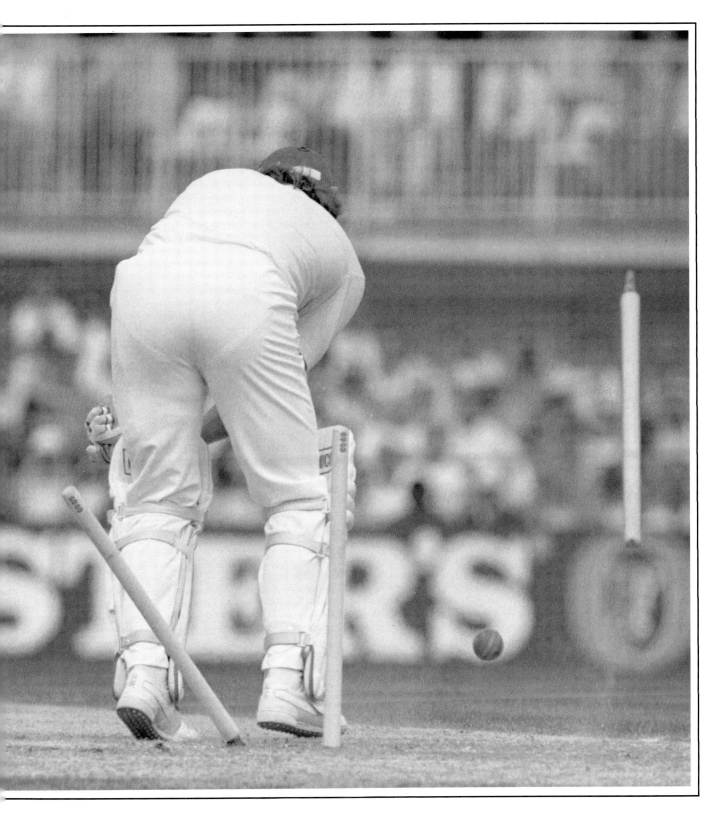

Sixth Test
The Oval

John Stephenson took a nasty one on the hand and needed prolonged treatment from the magic spray. He was just settling in, too. After this, he was out next ball to Alderman, caught at slip.

(Right) Not the most magical-looking of shots from Gower, but it was an innings all magic until he got out. He pulled, hooked, cut and drove with an airy lightness that most mortals only dream about. 'Cricket is a dance with a bat in the hand,' observed the monocled C. B. Fry once. Watching Gower in this mood one would certainly agree.

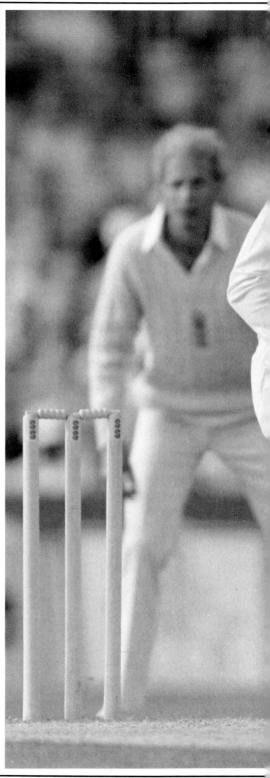

*Gladstone Small (far left) made 59 and looked good for many more. He drove
with such ease and flourish that it rather went to his head in the end, occasioning his
downfall.*

*Mark Taylor (left) settled in at the wicket as others do in a favourite armchair.
Never other than comfortable, he displayed such an air of familiarity and
occupation as Gooch might well have envied.*

*Even Taylor nodded occasionally (above), though usually through apparent
inattention rather than vulnerability. Here he followed one from Small that slanted
across him and Russell took a good catch.*

Sixth Test
The Oval

Since Atherton's bails (left) are already flying, Jones's appeal seems rather superfluous. Atherton, after his initial duck at Trent Bridge, batted with a becoming assurance, but sadly not for nearly long enough.

(Right) Robin Smith, yet again, stood between England and final humiliation. His 77 not out would probably not have saved the match without help from the weather, but it was gloriously defiant all the same.

The Ashes, or perhaps one of MCC's replicas.
Boon seems embarked on some esoteric ritual,
administering, perhaps, a kind of episcopal
blessing.

POSTSCRIPT

With so uneven a contest as these Tests turned out, it might be expected that they would lack tension or be downright boring. Curiously, this was never the case. There was, in the first instance, the continual fascination of observing a collection of individuals, many of them comparatively unfamiliar to English audiences or untutored in English conditions, develop into a highly organised side with no obvious weaknesses. It was well led, it worked hard, and it thrived on success.

At the other extreme there was England, increasingly in disarray and brutally hit by injuries. The Australian bowlers exposed the ineptness of the techniques of all the leading batsmen except for Robin Smith. Yet, as disaster followed disaster, there was a certain ghoulish interest in finding out what, if anything, could be salvaged from the series, and who by. Many high-scoring series, contested by evenly matched sides, have proved far less diverting. At least, during this series, there was always something happening, even if it was only the sound of English wickets falling.

From the moment that Gower, having won the toss, asked Australia to bat on the first morning, England were headed for trouble. Australia made 601 and on not one of the thirty days that followed did they fail to get the better of the play. That is remarkable enough in itself, and it is testimony to the continued pressure without let-up that Australia exerted.

They began as they meant to go on, with Taylor getting them off to the first of a sequence of affluent starts. Marsh, without often coming off, did his bit, and then the innings took on its familiar characteristics: Boon boisterous, Border canny, Jones arrogant, Waugh dismissive. If Taylor's flow of runs was something of a bonus for Border, it was the middle order that played up to and beyond expectation. Waugh treated the England bowling with contempt, and only in August did he lose something of his earlier invulnerability. Jones grew in stature and swagger with every match, a handsome player in all senses of the term.

With runs galore to play with in every match, Border was able to set attacking fields. He sized up each batsman's weakness in turn and placed his fielders accordingly. Alderman, at no great pace, but with infinite and minimal variations, trapped Gooch, first, and then those that partnered or followed him, in some kind of silken web in which they stumbled, all pads and fumble. Lawson, from Lord's onwards, found a rhythm and menace that reminded of his earliest days, though now aggression was tempered by intelligence. Hughes glared and thundered like some Victorian villain, moustaches aquiver and ears cocked for hisses, but he was an excellent foil whose bluff was only consistently called by Smith. Hohns was an unobtrusive leg-spinner who quickly settled on a length and made a second spinner a luxury Border could dispense with. Four bowlers were all he needed, so Waugh's comparative lack of penetration scarcely mattered. Had England even half-matched Australia for runs it could have been different.

Long before the series was over Gower looked a forlorn and rather tragic figure. He himself played four excellent innings, but there were too many failures in between, too apparently fatalistic an attitude towards dismissal. Gooch never got the hang of Alderman; Lamb, after a fine hundred, was out of the running; Botham had one injury after another; Broad, Robinson, Tavaré, Moxon and Barnett never quite looked the part; and Gatting at a crucial stage was hopelessly out of touch.

The batting in the end was carried by Robin Smith, with help from the ever-improving Russell. Smith, Russell, and Fraser were, in terms of the future, all England had to show for their efforts. Atherton, brought in for two Tests, may have the matter in him, and Hussain, picked for one Test but not played, almost certainly has.

Bobby Simpson, Australia's shrewd and observant coach, expressed himself astonished at the change that had come over English cricket: not just the decline in the quality of pitches, but the technical shortcomings of both bowlers and batsmen. 'Time and again,' Simpson remarked in a frank interview with Alan Lee of *The Times*, 'we saw England's batsmen make a half-forward movement with the foot not even pointing to the ball. It invites leg-before. And then there is the stance, the backlift and the use of heavy bats . . . Standing with your bat in the air destroys rhythm and balance . . . Our batters stand much easier at the crease. Our bats are also very much lighter and getting lighter all the time.' And so say all of us.

Australia have been down to the ocean bed in the last few years and now they have come up for air. Any batting side that can deal effectively with Alderman – as county sides have often done – will give them a run for their money, but it is going to take something out of the ordinary to bowl them out. West Indies have done it, but they may not find it so easy next time.

Practise makes perfect, they say; the Australians work at their game. English cricketers play too much, they are jaded and increasingly prone to injury, their appetite for the game seems dulled. The old gang is in decline, inured to defeat. When they are safely tucked up, English cricket will have to start afresh. A generation has been missed out, for one reason or another, so it will have to be with those who are only just coming into the county game, who have not yet picked up bad habits.

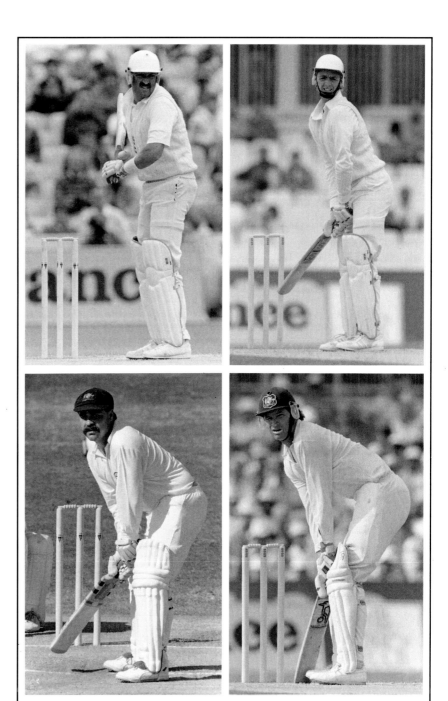

Nothing could better indicate the relative ease and consequent performance of the English and Australian batsmen than these studies. The two Australians, Boon and Jones, look relaxed and confident; the English, Gooch and Stephenson, with their awkward and ugly stances, bats aloft, very pictures of misery and tension. Their averages were Gooch 20, Stephenson 18, Boon 55, Jones 70.

England v. Australia
1989 Test Match Averages

AUSTRALIA

BATTING

	Matches	Inn's	Times Not Out	Runs	Highest Score	Average
S. R. Waugh	6	8	4	506	177★	126.0
M. A. Taylor	6	11	1	839	219	83.90
A. R. Border	6	9	3	442	80	73.66
D. M. Jones	6	9	1	566	157	70.75
D. C. Boon	6	11	3	442	94	55.25
T. V. Hohns	5	5	1	127	40	31.75
G. R. Marsh	6	11	0	347	138	31.54
G. F. Lawson	6	5	1	115	74	28.75
M. G. Hughes	6	5	0	127	71	25.40
T. M. Alderman	6	4	3	20	8	20.00
I. A. Healy	6	7	1	103	44	17.16

G.D. Campbell played in one match but did not bat.

BOWLING

	Overs	Maidens	Runs	Wickets	Average
T. M. Alderman	269.2	68	712	41	17.36
G. F. Lawson	277.1	76	791	29	27.27
T. V. Hohns	134.0	53	300	11	27.27
M. G. Hughes	189.2	41	515	19	32.36

Also bowled: A. R. Border 24-9-44-0; G. D. Campbell 24-0-124-1; S. R. Waugh 57-15-208-2.

HUNDREDS (7)
D. M. Jones (2): 157 (Edgbaston), 122 (Oval);
M. A. Taylor (2): 219 (Trent Bridge), 136 (Headingley);
S. R. Waugh (2): 177★ (Headingley), 152★ (Lord's);
G. R. Marsh: 138 (Trent Bridge)

Figures Courtesy Richard Lockwood

ENGLAND

BATTING

	Matches	Inn's	Times Not Out	Runs	Highest Score	Average
R. A. Smith	5	10	1	553	143	61.44
R. C. Russell	6	11	3	314	128★	39.25
D. I. Gower	6	11	0	383	106	34.81
J. E. Emburey	3	5	1	131	64	32.75
K. J. Barnett	3	5	0	141	80	28.20
N. G. B. Cook	3	5	3	45	31	22.50
G. R. Dilley	2	3	1	42	24	21.00
B. C. Broad	2	4	0	82	37	20.50
G. A. Gooch	5	9	0	183	68	20.33
M. A. Atherton	2	4	0	73	47	18.25
N. A. Foster	3	6	2	68	39	17.00
I. T. Botham	3	4	0	62	46	15.50
T. S. Curtis	3	5	0	71	41	14.20
D. R. Pringle	2	3	0	33	27	11.00
P. W. Jarvis	2	3	0	33	22	11.00
A. R. C. Fraser	3	5	0	47	29	9.40

Also batted: D. J. Capel, 4, 17; P. A. J. DeFreitas, 1, 21; M. W. Gatting, 0, 22; E. E. Hemmings, 38, 35; A. P. Igglesden, 2★; A. J. Lamb, 125, 4; D. E. Malcolm, 9, 5; M. D. Moxon, 0, 18; P. J. Newport, 36, 8; R. T. Robinson, 0, 12; G. C. Small, 59; J. P. Stephenson, 25, 11; C. J. Tavaré, 2.

BOWLING

	Overs	Maidens	Runs	Wickets	Average
N. A. Foster	154.0	42	421	12	35.08
A. R. C. Fraser	144.4	30	323	9	35.88
J. E. Emburey	152.0	37	342	8	42.75
A. P. Igglesden	37.0	3	146	3	48.66
G. C. Small	60.0	12	198	4	49.50
N. G. B. Cook	103.5	23	282	5	56.40
D. R. Pringle	86.2	12	306	5	61.20
G. R. Dilley	85.0	12	318	5	63.60
P. A. J. DeFreitas	63.3	10	216	3	72.00
I. T. Botham	80.0	15	241	3	80.33

Also bowled: M. A. Atherton 8-0-34-0; K. J. Barnett 6-0-32-0; D. J. Capel 24-2-101-2; T. S. Curtis 3-0-6-0; G. A. Gooch 29-8-71-1; D. E. Malcolm 44-2-166-1; E. E. Hemmings 33-9-81-0; P. J. Newport 44-7-175-2; P. W. Jarvis 69-2-290-2.

HUNDREDS (5)
R. A. Smith (2): 143 (Old Trafford), 101 (Trent Bridge); D. I. Gower: 106 (Lord's); A. J. Lamb: 125 (Headingley); R. C. Russell: 128★ (Old Trafford).